MW00638809

Pastor Cooney,

Let's get better together!

Pastor Brian

Eric Peterson's *Letters to a Young Pastor* is a must-read for every person in ministry . . . really, every Christ follower. In this collection of heartfelt letters from Eugene Peterson to his son, we get a look behind the curtain, a glimpse at the heart of one of our generation's most esteemed pastors. The letters reveal Eugene Peterson's passion for ministry, contemplative nature, and longing for authentic worship. He eloquently addresses the balance required of young pastors trying to maintain a strong family and marriage while dealing with the never-ending demands of clergy. Each turn of the page is filled with fresh insight and candid advice for the challenges every pastor faces—from the changes in society and technology to dealing with difficult people. Peterson has left behind a treasure chest of wisdom—don't miss out!

PALMER CHINCHEN, PHD, speaker; author of *Justice Calling*, *True Religion*, *Barefoot Tribe*, and *God Can't Sleep*

Letters to a Young Pastor is an amazing opportunity for you to be personally mentored by Eugene Peterson, one of the most significant spiritual leaders of our time. In this must-read book, Eric Peterson gives us a peek into the very special relationship he had with his father, Eugene, and in the process allows us to access to the wisdom that was passed down from one generation to the next. Every pastor and church leader, young and old, needs to read this book!

DAVE FERGUSON, lead pastor at Community Christian Church; author of *Hero Maker*

Preserving the words between a father and a son is priceless, especially when they are pastoral, brilliant, graced, and insightful. Herein we have Eugene the elder speaking to Eric the pastor, unlocking the keys to personal and pastoral identity with relational, theological, and incarnational wisdom. How kind of Eric to preserve these intimate and trusting letters for a wider audience. I'm refreshed by their authenticity and blessed by their depth.

STEPHEN A. MACCHIA, founder and president of Leadership Transformations; author of fifteen books, including *Legacy*, *Crafting a Rule of Life*, and *Becoming a Healthy Church*

From the days of Aaron, the Lord has preserved a priestly line. Such lines are always preserved by the transference of wisdom from one generation to the next, so having Eugene and Eric Peterson's letters in our hands is a gift. They are tender and thoughtful, witty and wise, and you will be the better for reading them. This family continues to shape the pastoral imagination in America.

DANIEL GROTHE, pastor at New Life Church; author of *Chasing Wisdom*

LETTERS

— *to a* —

YOUNG

PASTOR

Timothy conversations between father and son

ERIC E. PETERSON
EUGENE H. PETERSON

A NavPress resource published in alliance
with Tyndale House Publishers

NavPress is the publishing ministry of The Navigators, an international Christian organization and leader in personal spiritual development. NavPress is committed to helping people grow spiritually and enjoy lives of meaning and hope through personal and group resources that are biblically rooted, culturally relevant, and highly practical.

For more information, visit NavPress.com.

Letters to a Young Pastor: Timothy Conversations between Father and Son

Copyright © 2020 by Eric E. Peterson. All rights reserved.

A NavPress resource published in alliance with Tyndale House Publishers

NAVPRESS and the NavPress logo are registered trademarks of NavPress, The Navigators, Colorado Springs, CO. *TYNDALE* is a registered trademark of Tyndale House Publishers. Absence of ® in connection with marks of NavPress or other parties does not indicate an absence of registration of those marks.

The Team:
Don Pape, Publisher
David Zimmerman, Acquisitions Editor
Elizabeth Schroll, Copy Editor
Ron Kaufmann, Designer

Cover illustration of shepherd copyright © duncan1890/iStockphoto. All rights reserved.

Cover and interior illustration of landscape copyright © VladisChern/Depositphotos. All rights reserved.

Author photograph by Chadwick Gantes, copyright © 2016. All rights reserved.

Unless otherwise indicated, all Scripture quotations are taken from the Revised Standard Version of the Bible, copyright © 1952 [2nd edition, 1971] by the Division of Christian Education of the National Council of the Churches of Christ in the United States of America. Used by permission. All rights reserved. Scripture quotations marked KJV are taken from the *Holy Bible*, King James Version. Scripture quotations marked NIV are taken from the Holy Bible, *New International Version,*® *NIV.*® Copyright © 1973, 1978, 1984, 2011 by Biblica, Inc.® Used by permission. All rights reserved worldwide. Scripture quotations marked NRSV are taken from the New Revised Standard Version Bible, copyright © 1989, Division of Christian Education of the National Council of the Churches of Christ in the United States of America. Used by permission. All rights reserved.

The anecdotal illustrations in this book are true to life and are included with the permission of the persons involved.

For information about special discounts for bulk purchases, please contact Tyndale House Publishers at csresponse@tyndale.com, or call 1-800-323-9400.

ISBN 978-1-64158-111-0

Printed in the United States of America

26	25	24	23	22	21	20
7	6	5	4	3	2	1

―――

Dedicated to the women and men who carry on the noble work of pastoral ministry.

―――

CONTENTS

INTRODUCTION

——

IT WAS A BIG SKY DAY in the summer of 1980 as my dad and I made the round-trip drive from Lakeside, Montana, to Spokane, Washington. Ostensibly, the purpose of the trip was to visit Whitworth University to see if it might be a good fit for a liberal-arts education. (It was, and I spent three delightful and deeply formative years on its campus.) However, as is often the case, there were purposes beyond purposes; the presenting opportunity to check out a college led to something much more significant and durable. Namely, it was the seed for a deepening relationship that would develop between a father and a son.

The eight hours we spent in the car together created an undistracted container for continual conversation that spanned a broad range of topics. I forget many of the details of that day from many years ago, but I do recall that we talked about geography, particularly the glacial carvings from the last ice age and the Great Missoula Flood, both of which shaped the topography of that area—slowly in the former case, rapidly in the latter. We spoke of love and relationships;

I was in love with a beautiful girl who had just moved away, and I was feeling the sting of separation. And we talked about the prophet Jeremiah, with whom I had come to identify, both because he was called by God as a young man and because his dad was a pastor. That part of the conversation led Eugene to preach a sermon series the next fall which later developed into *Run with the Horses*, the book he dedicated to "Eric, also the son of a priest."[1]

The next morning, while swimming together in Flathead Lake, I told him how much I had enjoyed the previous day and asked if we could find a way to continue the conversations when we got home. Once we returned to Maryland that fall, we had a standing date. Every Tuesday afternoon during my senior year of high school, I rode my bicycle to his study at our church. The pattern was simple: We read a paragraph from one of the Pastoral Epistles, using it as a springboard to reflect on our respective ministries (I was involved with Young Life at the time), and we prayed. Our "Timothy conversations," we called them.

Sixteen years later, I found myself in the intense and demanding environment of the first year of a church plant. Although I had gone to good schools and received a solid theological education, I had learned nearly nothing about organizing a church from scratch. I was overwhelmed. I felt incompetent. Failure was a frequent fear. Secretly, I was quite sure that they had called the wrong guy. On a whim, I picked up the phone and called the only person I trusted to guide me through the maze. "Dad, I've been ordained for seven years, and I still feel like I don't know what I'm doing.

Would you write me some letters, reflecting on the pastoral vocation?"

During the brief pause on the other end of the line, I imagined that he might say something like "Actually, I've written several books on pastoral theology; you might read those." Instead, he unreservedly said, "Sure!" as if he had just been standing by, waiting for the phone to ring.

His enthusiastic response to the proposal immediately reminded me of a moment in my teen years. It was a season of life when I was doing my own thing and he was doing his own thing, but we were doing precious little of it together. But one afternoon, I walked through the front door of the house to find him lying on the sofa, reading a thick volume of Barth's *Church Dogmatics*. I sat down in a chair opposite him, and he immediately popped upright, slammed the book closed, and pushed it aside. He then leaned in, giving me his full attention for whatever I might have to say. He didn't even mark the page. It was as if he were killing time with a dead German theologian, just waiting for me to show up.

His response to me from the other end of the phone that day, three Northwest states away, felt much the same, as if he had just been frittering away his time, waiting for an invitation to enter my life, my world.

And so began the intentional correspondence in which we reflected together on the pastoral vocation. "Timothy Letters," we called them. Like Paul writing to the younger pastor, his "true son in the faith,"[2] letters full of advice, encouragement, and mentoring with respect to the pastoral life.

Over the course of his long life and ministry—it's

impossible to refer to one without the other—Eugene preached a lot of sermons, delivered a lot of lectures, and wrote a lot of books. Lots and lots of words can be found in the wake of his life. But to be in a conversation with Eugene Peterson was to get the man at his best. Whatever else might be said about him, he was inherently relational. His life was grounded in the doctrine of the Incarnation: In matters of salvation and liberation, everything is getting worked out in the context of relationships—life in the flesh, life together in community. To have a leisurely hour or two over a meal, to sit with him and to engage in an uninterrupted conversation . . . well, there's nothing quite like it. However, that not always being possible, a correspondence in letters was the next best thing. For most of my adult years, I never lived closer than a four-hour drive from him. But the letters we exchanged became the continuation of our less frequent face-to-face conversations. Moreover, that we had to settle for letter writing because of distance resulted in a preservation of words that would have, otherwise, been lost.

In 1929, Franz Kappus published a collection of ten letters he had received, over a period of five years (1903–1908), from the esteemed writer and philosopher Rainer Maria Rilke. *Letters to a Young Poet*, as they are now known to us, are personal, brilliant, insightful, even pastoral. But we only get one side of the correspondence, and the reader is required to infer what was written from the missing side of the exchange. As if to explain why he omitted his own part of the conversation, Kappus, in his introduction, wrote, "When a truly great and unique spirit speaks, the lesser ones must be silent."[3]

What follows, with only minor edits, are thirty-seven letters from the greater side of a ten-year correspondence which, I believe, may have some lasting wisdom for other younger or older pastors who need the steadying guidance from a sage. Eugene H. Peterson was my dad. But he was also the holiest man I have either known or known of. His life formed me to be the person and pastor I am more than I would even venture to guess. I hope that, in the pages that follow, you will allow the legacy of his enduring spirit to converse with you, as well.

Eric Eugene Peterson
Pentecost, 2020

TIMELINE

—

1962–1991	Eugene founded and served Christ Our King Presbyterian Church in Bel Air, MD.
1963	Eric was born in Bel Air, MD.
1976	Eugene published his first book: *Growing Up with Your Teenager* (later retitled as *Like Dew Your Youth*).
1980	Eugene published *A Long Obedience in the Same Direction: Discipleship in an Instant Society* (InterVarsity Press) and *Five Smooth Stones for Pastoral Work* (John Knox).
1981	Eric graduated from Bel Air High School.
1983	Eugene dedicated *Run with the Horses: The Quest for Life at Its Best* (InterVarsity Press) to Eric, "also the son of a priest."
1985	Eric graduated from Whitworth University in Spokane, WA.

1990	Eric graduated from Princeton Theological Seminary and was ordained.
1990–1997	Eric served as associate pastor at Marine View Presbyterian Church in Tacoma, WA.
1991–1992	Eugene was a visiting professor at Pittsburgh Seminary, where he translated much of the New Testament.
1993–1998	Eugene served as the James M. Houston Professor of Spiritual Theology at Regent College in Vancouver, BC.
1993	Eugene published *The Message: The New Testament in Contemporary Language* (NavPress) and *The Contemplative Pastor: Returning to the Art of Spiritual Direction* (Eerdmans).
1997–present	Eric founded and served Colbert Presbyterian Church in eastern Washington.
1998	Eugene and Jan retired to Flathead Lake in Montana.
1999	Eugene and Eric began the correspondence that follows in this book.
2000	Eugene published *The Unnecessary Pastor: Rediscovering the Call* (Eerdmans), coauthored with Marva Dawn—the first of his books to be published during his correspondence with Eric.
2001	Eugene contributed two lectures, on "The Gift of Time" and "The Gift of Place," to the Regent

College lecture series "Creation & Gospel: From the Garden to the Ends of the Earth."

2002 Eugene completed his translation of the Old Testament, publishing the full text of *The Message* (NavPress).

2005 Leif Peterson (Eric's brother) published his novel *Catherine Wheels* (Waterbrook).

2005–2010 Eugene published his Eerdmans series on spiritual theology: *Christ Plays in Ten Thousand Places: A Conversation in Spiritual Theology* (2005); *Eat This Book: A Conversation in the Art of Spiritual Reading* (2006); *The Jesus Way: A Conversation on the Ways that Jesus Is the Way* (2007); *Tell It Slant: A Conversation on the Language of Jesus in His Stories and Prayers* (2008); and *Practice Resurrection: A Conversation on Growing Up in Christ* (2010).

2006 Eugene published *Living the Resurrection: The Risen Christ in Everyday Life* (NavPress).

2011 Eugene published *The Pastor: A Memoir* (HarperOne).

2018 Eric published *Wade in the Water: Following the Sacred Stream of Baptism* (Cascade).

2018 Eugene died Monday, October 22, in Lakeside, MT.

2019 Jan died Friday, May 10, in Kalispell, MT.

THE FIRST LETTER

———

Christmas Day 1999

Dear Eric,

    I can't tell you how pleased I've been since you suggested that I write these letters to you, reflecting on our common pastoral calling. (Jan is too!) And I've been writing and rewriting (in my head) this first one ever since your telephone call, trying to get it right. And I can't. I guess I'm thinking I've got to come up with something like Paul to Timothy and Titus. And I can't—so this is what you get—just your old dad, trying to make sense of what we've both been given to do.

    I think what strikes me most forcibly as I go over this is how different your world is from the one I grew up in and tried to learn how to be a pastor in. And in the light of that, realizing how context-specific pastoral work is: There is not much that can be generalized and passed on from one generation to another. The substance, of course, is the same—prayer and the Scriptures, obedient love and the holy sacraments, honest preaching and teaching. But the details—and pastoral work is almost nothing but details—are so different that practically everything has to be worked out from scratch, on the job. People's expectations, their views of what is involved in marriage and parenting, and their attitudes toward work and jobs, music and worship, the use of money and nature of commitments—all of these things and more are not totally different, but just enough so that leading people into a life of worship and discipleship requires paying attention to all these details so that we don't impose a spirituality on them from without but develop it from within.

Something, for instance, as simple and common (now) as the Internet throws a monkey wrench into the works by almost totally depersonalizing knowledge, reducing it to a cataract of mere information. This reduction of knowledge to information has always been possible, and the forces that exacerbate it have been growing ever since Gutenberg, but now, with the prevalence of quick access to virtually everything there is to know, the link between person and knowledge is, if not destroyed, at least weakened to an extent that is most troubling. Knowledge is less a personal exchange and more a commodity than ever before. And that makes it more difficult to preach the gospel and teach the Scriptures and direct personal growth than ever before—more difficult for you, I think, than for me.

I don't think for a minute this is new, but the scale is new, and it is that scale which affects pastoral work. The area where I notice it most is in what people unconsciously look for in their pastor: The pastor is not one to whom we look for knowledge or truth; the pastoral office is perceived in emotional terms—feelings of reassurance and comfort, a source of inspiration and good cheer, a figure of advocacy.

One of the great elements of distinction in the pastoral office is that it is personal. Everything—administration, teaching, healing, counsel—is represented in a named person who people can listen to and touch, speak the pastor's name and expect the pastor to speak their name. But when this personal dimension is then reduced to merely functional and emotional areas, the implicit authority of the office is diminished greatly.

I've reflected on this in the matter of Melody.[1] This might not be the best example, since I don't know the details. And if I have it wrong, just censor this

out. But my outsider impression is that Melody was
brought into your ministry with a great deal of personal
attention; early misunderstandings were worked out in
a lot of detail; there was a great deal of investment in
relationship as you took her into your confidence in what
the leadership of worship involved and what working
with those worship leaders means. Lynn[2] worked hard
at this, setting herself aside and working for a common
good. And then the whole thing falls apart because
she understands her basic place in that worshipping
community as a matter of status and money, and these
function entirely apart from personal relationships. The
most telling detail for me was in her threat to hire a
lawyer and take the matter to a civil court. That kind
of conflict is not so unusual, but I think the volatility,
the quick fuse, the seemingly total absence on her
part of relationship with you and the congregation—I
think that is a sign that assumptions have changed
considerably. The overwhelming context out of which
she is working has to do with function and status and
money—depersonalized categories. As we live in a world
of the Internet (and related phenomena), this kind of
thing happens more and more.

It is the pastor, whose work is nothing if not personal,
and whose God is nothing if not personal, who is at the
front line of experiencing this shift in sensibility and

has to be thinking strategically all the time, devising language and approaches to counter it.

The good news is that the pastor in the congregation is probably in the most effective place in the world to counter these cultural demons. The act of Sunday worship, the access to homes, the almost total lack of commercial and commodity considerations in your work, the cultural "uselessness" of your work—all these put you in an enviable and strategic way of life to develop a community in which people discover and develop lives that are lived in response to the God who reveals himself in Jesus and works by the Holy Spirit to customize every part of the revelation of salvation and holiness to the uniqueness of each person.

Well, this is some of what I've been thinking about on Christmas morning as I am appreciating the way you pursue your calling and praying for wisdom and grace for you this week.

THE SECOND LETTER

—

16 January 2000
Second Sunday in Epiphany

Dear Eric,

Sunday morning and you're getting ready to lead your congregation in worship—present them to God, present God to them. I woke up early this morning, thinking, in my half-sleep state, that I was going to do it myself; out of a tangle of dreams, I was trying to get my sermon into focus, anticipating being in the Christ Our King sanctuary. And then I was fully awake, with a feeling of letdown. That doesn't happen very often, but when it does, I compensate by thinking about you entering your pulpit in Colbert, in your praying and preaching.

I've been working hard the last month on talks I'm going to give to The Navigators this week at Glen

Eyrie—and then again at Regent in the spring. I think I've told you something about this—the idea for the subject came during our trip to Israel last year at this time: Follow the Leader.[1] I've had to work harder on these lectures than I anticipated, but I'm glad I had it to do, for it has given me occasion to work through a lot of what I have lived through pastorally.

One of the irritants that got me going in this was my sense that one of the primary seductions to pastoral faithfulness and integrity these days is this drumbeat of emphasis—throughout church and society—on *leadership*. All these books and conferences and tapes on leadership—how to be an effective leader, a successful leader, a powerful leader. Leadership distilled to technique and strategy and method. And much of it—maybe most—good and useful. But so much of it has little to do with what it means to be a pastor.

Every pastor is subjected to these images and counsel and advice constantly, unremittingly. Maybe a new church pastor is especially vulnerable to it, since so much depends on what you are doing—you don't have several generations of congregational tradition and leadership backing you up. And so I think of you a lot as I've been going over all this stuff, the minefield that you are picking your way through as you work with those people in the formation of a church of Jesus Christ.

My renewed conviction is that pastoral leadership is, as the scholars say, *sui generis*, absolutely unique. It is in a different category entirely from what goes on in a business or school or corporation. Barth and Bonhoeffer made a big thing out of the uniqueness of the Christian congregation—that baptism (which you've been dealing with so much the last couple of years and to such good effect) creates an identity that can't be subsumed under any of the usual sociological categories for understanding people. Well, I think the same thing goes for pastoral identity.

We get out of bed each morning and pray, "Lord Jesus Christ, I follow you. I deny myself, I take up my cross, and I follow you." Our basic identity is not leader but follower. Jesus never tells us to lead; he invites us to follow. Followership is previous to and more comprehensive than leadership.

Ray, who led our Israel group last year, made a big thing of "following the rabbi." He said it was an old, old tradition—he was sure going back into pre-Christian Galilee. The subject came up because people in our group were always saying, "Ray, what are we going to do today? Where are we going? When are we going to have lunch? Why are we going up this trail?" And Ray wouldn't answer—he just ignored the questions. And then, once in a while, he would say something like, "Listen,

I know where I'm going. Trust me. If I tell you ahead
of time what we're doing, where we're going, you start
forming ideas in your mind that will be wrong—walking
by faith involves an openness to seeing, hearing what you
don't know, can't anticipate. Follow the rabbi, let the
rabbi do it his way, with his sense of timing. Trust him
to make the right decisions along the way and get you
where he wants you to go." And I remembered how often
Jesus didn't answer questions.

So I reflect on this in the swirl of leadership talk.
If our leadership involves clear and focused "vision
statements" and "attainable goals"—if it means an
obsession with knowing where we are going, our aptitude
for following atrophies. If our primary identity is
"leader," we marginalize our "follower" status, which is
the only thing Jesus seemed to care about with us.

And the point is that as followers, we don't know that
much about what is ahead. We just don't. Jerusalem, yes.
But Jesus' followers had hardly any idea of what that was
going to involve.

So here's what I have been doing as I've tried to
understand what we pastors are doing in this "leadership"
world in which we're trying to maintain our previous
and primary identity as followers. I've taken three
prominent leaders in the first century and contrasted
them with Jesus: Herod, Caiaphas, and Josephus. They

range themselves in a nicely symmetrical schema: Herod at Jesus' birth, Caiaphas at Jesus' death, and Josephus in the world of Jesus' resurrection. Herod, the powerful politician who virtually defined the world in which Jesus grew up. Caiaphas, the most prominent religious leader, who controlled the Temple establishment and worship. Josephus, the consummate opportunist who was a brilliant success, first as a Jewish diplomat and general and then as a Roman military leader and writer, wheeling and dealing his way to the top at the very same time that Paul was in prison and the Christian church was struggling to survive at the margins of society.

The striking thing to me is that at the end of the first century (Herod died at the beginning of the century, and Josephus died in AD 100), those three leaders were the most admired and most successful. I think they still are. Jesus is better known now, celebrated and honored. But he is not much followed: Herod, Caiaphas, and Josephus are the models for leadership, both inside and outside of the church, that are most frequently emulated.

And here's another interesting thing: All three of those leaders operated in the context of protest/reform movements out of Judaism: the Pharisees were the protest/reform movement against Herodianism; the Essenes against the Caiaphas/Sadducee domination of Temple worship; and the Zealots in contrast to Josephus.

All three protest/reform movements were strong and
effective in their own ways—and had many good and
admirable people in them. But Jesus did not join any
of them. He did something unique—neither "for" nor
"against" the big names.

This accentuates the uniqueness of Jesus in the
conditions in which he worked and the conditions in
which we follow him.

He didn't shape his leadership (and we don't acquire
our followership) by paying too close attention to what
the world is doing, or to the protests against what the
world is doing. Jesus is unique. Pastoral "followership" is
unique. We have to do it in the world of Herod-Caiaphas-
Josephus and the world of Pharisee-Essene-Zealot but
not let them define us. Jesus was very much immersed in
that world, but he simply went about his work, revealing
God to us, inaugurating the Kingdom, and inviting us to
follow him.

The complicating factor in all of this for pastors is
that much of what these leadership models provide us is
good and right—and we can't help, if we are going to get
on with our work, employing a lot of it. But how do we
use what we need to use without getting defined by it,
without becoming any of those identities?

What I am feeling—and this is so much of what I have
felt from the day of ordination—is that very few people

are helping us understand the absolute uniqueness of the way Jesus leads us in this world.

Anyway, getting inside the first-century Jesus world in the conditions of three leaders and three reform movements has been good for me and has given me a lot to think about, both for myself and in relation to you as you make decisions that incrementally form both your pastoral and congregational identities: the decisions about architecture and finances, the details of worship and mission, parenthood and husbandhood. And I think it is incremental: We don't make big decisions and then work from there; the decisions are in the details that add up to something we don't know much about yet. The followership thing again.

Jan and I leave Wednesday for Glen Eyrie, where I'll deliver these lectures to mostly laity—men and women who think of themselves (I am guessing) as the movers and shakers of the evangelical world. I wonder how they'll receive them.

Leif and Amy and Hans and Anna are coming for dinner after church (leg of lamb!), and we anticipate a couple of hours of cross-country skiing first.

With love + in prayer
Dad

THE THIRD LETTER

---

23 February 2000

Dear Eric,

Another Timothy Letter. We are leaving in the morning for Bel Air and Christ Our King for a few days. As I have been preparing myself, both in what I will say and preach but also emotionally, I have thought a lot of those years—so formative. Interestingly, mostly what I feel is a kind of messiness: What a lot of stumbling around, fumbling the ball, losing my way went on through those years. It is amazing to me now that anything came of it.

Which leads me to reflect on the uniqueness of being a pastor—being a pastor is unique. Not better, not privileged, not anything special, but unique in society as a whole—and also (but not quite so much) in the company of the people of God. Not much transfers from other vocational roles to who we are, what we do.

One aspect of that uniqueness, I think, is that we make far more mistakes in our line of work than other so-called professionals. If physicians and engineers and lawyers and military officers made as many mistakes as we do in our line of work, they would be out on the street in no time. It amazes me still how much of the time I simply don't know what I am doing, don't know what to say, don't know what the next move is. The temptation in that state of being is to become competent at something or other—master something or someone. Unfortunately, there are many opportunities, many "ways of escape" in which we can exercise and develop areas of administrative or leadership or scholarly or programmatic competencies in the church.

But I had a sense much of the time (but not by any means continuously) that "not knowing what I am doing" is more or less what it feels like when I am "trusting in God" and "following Jesus." This position, in which the church has placed us by ordaining us to this work, means giving witness to what we don't know much about, living into the mystery of salvation and providence.[1]

I just thought of a phrase that I have sometimes lingered on: "Blessed is the man who makes the LORD his trust, who does not turn to the proud, to those who go astray after false gods."[2] The "proud" for me in this context are just those people who look like they know what they're doing—who are competent and recognized as such, who have an honored position in society and among their colleagues. And going "astray after false gods" amounts to living in response to something manageable, turning my vocation into a job that I can get good at. I'm probably reading more into this text than it warrants, but it has given me a couple of images ("proud" and "astray") that set off little alarm signals when I sense that I am betraying or avoiding the uniqueness of "pastor."

The odd thing, the surprising thing from this perspective as I reflect on those thirty years, is that I have almost no sense of achievement—what I remember is all the little detours into "proud" and "astray" that I experienced, the near misses, the staggering recoveries or semi-recoveries of who I was and what I was about. In a couple of days, we are going to be back in that place, and everybody is going to be celebrating those years—they'll have no idea how precarious it felt at the time, how many faithless stretches there were, how uncelebrative it felt for so much of the time.

In retrospect now, the two things that preserved for me the uniqueness of "pastor" were worship and marriage/family. I knew in my gut that that act of worship every week was what kept me centered and that nothing could be permitted to dilute it or distract from it. And I knew that marriage/family were the only hope I had of staying grounded, faithful, relational, learning the practice of love: Jan and you kids provided the conditions in which I could be a pastor.

Maybe those things don't make "pastor" unique—everybody has to deal with them. But we are very public in what we do in relation to God and love. And that, if not unique, is at least intense, providing occasion for either bluffing our way or constructing a way of life that is "competent" but quite apart from trusting God or braving the intimacies of love. Everybody sees and is influenced either for good or bad by the seriousness and reverence in which we order our response to God (the showcase for it is Sunday worship), and they all notice the way we live with our spouse and kids—they see or don't see forgiveness and grace and blessing and patience in all our gestures and offhand remarks.

And the daily, inescapable reality is that neither one of these areas, worship or family, are we ever in control of, or can manage; if we try, we end up being self-conscious, substituting our ego and performance and reputation for the very things we are committed to doing—worshipping God, loving our spouse and kids.

I wish you and Lynn and Drew and Lindsay and Sadie were going back with us this weekend. I'd like to show you off. I think you might make me feel competent in that place for once.

Your proud Dad

THE FOURTH LETTER

—

5 April 2000

Fourth Week in Lent

Dear Eric,

I spent last Saturday evening at Gig Harbor. I found myself immersed in "Eric Territory." It seemed like every other person I met mentioned you. I liked it.

The evening also plunged me into a kind of tension or polarity that I never get used to, the identification with the world of loss and limit and pain and rejection and suffering (the world that Search is attending to),[1] and the world of order and prosperity and success and reward and security and achievement (the world that Mitchell, pastor of the church at Gig Harbor, seems to epitomize, almost to the point of parody). The pastoral task, it seems to me, is to live in both worlds at the same time, amphibiously.

But it sure isn't easy. One seems to exclude the other, and
I feel I have to choose. It's tempting to throw your lot in
on one side or the other—and that is certainly right for
some people. But it never was for me, and I sense that
you are not leaning that way either. I don't want to hog
the term *pastor* for the definitions I put into it, but my
sense is that pastor in the generic sense is this amphibious
creature, learning how to become at home in both worlds,
not only the biblical and contemporary but the various
"worlds" that people inhabit economically and socially
and culturally.

I've liked the way you keep coming back to baptism
as providing the rock-bottom definition of the people
you are dealing with. I've heard you bring the term
up several times in the last couple of years in different
contexts, and it always sounds so right. It prevents us
from taking on reductive sociological and demographic
and psychological labels for people. It keeps us mindful
that we are dealing with *souls*, not consumers or achievers
or victims or whatever.

Some of this reflection was fed by our trip back to
Christ Our King in February. I didn't really know what
to expect, but what happened was very good. Some of
this I know I've told you before, but let me go over
some old ground again. When we went to Bel Air, I had
never lived in a suburb. Small town (Kalispell) and cities

(Seattle, New York, Baltimore) had been my homes. I
was initially excited and energized by the chance to
be in on the development of a new congregation, but
after a few months, I began to be appalled by the way
of life of these people—they all seemed so atrophied, so
security conscious, so blended into a stereotype. There
were no sharp edges, no engaging conversations, no
differences—all the houses were being built to the same
basic blueprint, but also the conversations and the
social activities. They seemed to have settled for so
little. And here I was preaching/teaching the Kingdom
of God, which seemed to me a radical piece of good
news, something *large*. But they translated it back
immediately into the world in which they were hoping
to be comfortable and retire in security. I didn't know
if I could last very long. It seemed impossible to get a
hearing for the gospel in that context.

I was reading a lot of John Henry Newman those
days. After his conversion to Rome at about age forty, he
decided to establish an Oratory, a foundation of a few
men who would work in the city. He chose Birmingham,
an industrial, blue-collar place. All his friends objected—
he was the most prominent Christian intellectual in
England, the best writer, the best preacher—virtually
the best everything. And here he was going into the
obscurity and dullness and cultural/intellectual waste

of Birmingham, giving his life to these unpromising
people. In a letter to one of these objectors, he wrote,
"Birmingham people also have souls."[2] That hit me hard.
Yes, Bel Air suburbanites also have souls. It was a little
miniconversion, and I started redefining every one of
these people as a "soul." It had the same effect on me as
your insistence on seeing each person as baptized.

It took Jan and me a while, but slowly, we learned
to set aside our boredom and criticism and distaste for
the kind of lives they were living and deal with souls. I
realized that suburbia may be the most godless segment
of the population in the whole world—the most pressing
missionary field—and settled in to making it my lifework.

All this came flooding back to me as we returned to
Christ Our King. It was like we had never been gone—the
reconnection was immediate. All these so ordinary people,
but each one interesting, with a history of suffering and
struggle and worship and sin and salvation that turned
out to be absolutely unique. Now, after the separation of
nine years, I could see something of what happened as
these people were treated through those years for what
they really were, not what the culture did to them or what
they thought of themselves but as souls. They weren't
used to that, and when we came back to them, they were
responding, I think, to that experience, that relationship.
They weren't used to being treated with the dignity of

"souls"—they were used to being treated as consumers or as victims, exploited and/or condescended to.

The sense of community that returned almost immediately surprised both of us, for none of these people meant much to us personally as friends. We didn't miss them when we left. And coming back, I didn't sense any sentimentality in them, that they had been pining for us or felt bereft of us. No, it was this intimacy that was a result of being treated as souls, and it was simply there, as strong as ever. It was as if we had walked back into a company of people with no sense of break or interruption. The little kids had grown up, everyone was grayer, and the old people had shrunk considerably. A surprising number had gotten fat, which has something to do, I think, with being blessed—the "weight of glory." But nothing else had changed—it was like being plunged into a sea of intimacy and gratitude.

And I've thought about that since. I wonder if one of the greatest things that a pastor can do (after the basics are in place—the preaching and praying and teaching; staying true to God and following Jesus) is to treat men and women with simple dignity. That act in itself perhaps does all that needs to be done to bridge the worlds of need and affluence, rejection and acceptance, suffering and prosperity, failure and achievement. We aren't devising strategies on community or evangelism or mission, but on something far more basic—baptism/image of God/souls. The dignity of souls created by God. Virtually nobody in our culture does that, whether in or out of the church; they are reduced to consumers and "resources" and victims— defined by their problems or their status or their function. We pastors at least have the context and vocabulary in which we can treat them with the dignity of souls.

It does distress me when I hear pastors referring to their parishioners in functional and impersonal terms. And I hear it a lot, and you do, too; it's endemic to the clergy culture.

Combining the Gig Harbor visit and the Christ Our King visit, that's what I've been thinking of: the unique pastoral position of having an entire Kingdom context and vocabulary for meeting and dealing with people in this personal, honoring, welcoming, dignity-conferring way, regardless of who they are or how they are used to seeing themselves or being treated.

The sun is shining today—or at least it was up until a half hour ago—and I'm headed up to my workshop to work on a toy for Anna for her birthday in a couple of weeks.

You'll be thrilled to know that I am now translating Leviticus. I know you are anticipating that, and you no doubt have your whole congregation waiting in anticipation. If you want to plan your next series of sermons on Leviticus, I'll prepare a special pre-publication package for you to work on.

I love you a lot, Eric, and I treasure these times to have pastor talk with you.

Dad

THE FIFTH LETTER

—

11 May 2000

Dear Eric,

My sense is that you are more fortunate than I ever was in having pastoral colleagues, peers among whom you feel congenial. Or maybe it is not a matter of "fortunate" at all; maybe you're just better at it. At least one factor in this is that you grew up Presbyterian, and I didn't. I never felt totally and naturally at home among the Presbyterians. I can't put my finger on it exactly; much of it has to do with emotional memories that accumulate through childhood and adolescence and give structure to your perceptions.

I'm reflecting on this right now because we spent several days with all the Lutheran pastors of Montana

the week after Easter at Chico Hot Springs, a resort
down by Yellowstone Park. They do this every year at
this time, and this year, they invited us down.

It was a good week with them—congenial, easy, and
relaxed. Our pastor at Eidsvold was the only one I knew,
although I had met a few others. They were appreciative
of what I did, and the two other leaders—one a preacher
and the other a professor from Concordia Seminary—
worked well together. So everything that you can evaluate
and give marks to was about as good as it can get.

But why didn't I feel at home? Why didn't I fit into
the "club"? I liked these people; they liked me—why
don't I relish the company of fellow pastors? And it
isn't just Lutherans or Presbyterians; I get this sense
whenever I am with gatherings of men and women with
religious jobs (including at Regent, although I had that
feeling least there). And that, I think, might be the clue.
Anyway, I am going to try this out on you.

I'm guessing that it might be the irreverence. I half
expect but never quite get a sense of the holy, of awe,
of what our psalmists and prophets name "the fear of
the LORD." The times of worship were good at Chico—
Lutherans are great singers—but they did not seem to
permeate the rest of the day. There is a general sense
of the flip or the superficial; there is a lot of shoptalk.
Ecclesiastical politics seem to be on virtually everyone's

agenda, even though not very high up on the agenda for a lot of them. The level of chatter seems excessively high.

The world of professional or institutional religion doesn't seem to me to be either very personal or very reverent. The more we handle holy words and holy things, the less we are aware of the numinous, the holy, the exuberant action of the Trinity that is the context for all that we do and are.

Now that Jan and I are in this quiet and more personal place, I am not weighed down by these things, but when I return, like at Chico for a few days, all the feelings of those years of alienation and lack of intimacy come back.

I don't know what to do about it. What do *you* do about it? The main thing, I suppose, is not to join the professional/religious club. To maintain a certain detachment from it, for the minute those assumptions—that world of appearance and performance—become internalized, we are sunk. But how to do that while still being open and receiving and compassionate with our colleagues requires constant attention. Aloofness is not the answer. Detachment, in the old monastic sense, is more like it. For detachment means that we maintain an intimate involvement and engagement but give up all control or concern about what happens or what people think of us. Dorotheus of Gaza, the sixth-century monk, described detachment as "being free from wanting certain things to happen" and remaining so trusting of God that "what is happening will be the thing you want and you will be at peace with all."[1]

Detachment may be the most important factor in maintaining a sense of reverence, an attentiveness to the holy God and the holy souls around us, while living vocationally in the noise and clanking of gears in the ecclesiastical machinery of church and denomination.

And I didn't quite maintain the detachment that I value so much. But I heard a lot of Lutheran jokes those days. Here are a few I remember:

A pastor, upon retiring, was going through his closets, sorting out stuff. He was cleaning out his daughter's closet and came upon a shoebox with three eggs and one hundred one-dollar bills in it. He showed his wife and said, "Our daughter forgot to take this when she moved out."

His wife said, "Oh, that's not hers, that's mine."

He said, "What are the eggs for?"

She said, "You don't want to know."

He pressed her, saying, "After forty-five years of marriage, are you going to keep secrets from me?"

She relented. "When you became a pastor, I decided that every time your sermon bombed, when you laid an egg in the pulpit, I would put an egg in the shoe box."

He said, "Well, that's not bad, three eggs in forty-five years. What are the one hundred one-dollar bills for?"

She said, "You don't want to know."

He pressed her. She relented. "Well, when I got a dozen eggs, I sold them to the neighbors for a dollar."

A pastor found a dead mule on his front lawn and called up the county officials to do something about it.

The official said, "I thought you people took care of the dead."

He said, "Yes, we do, but we always notify the next of kin first."

A school was having problems with bats—bats everywhere. They couldn't get rid of them. The principal called up the Lutheran pastor. He came out and confirmed the bats, and they were never seen again.

A retiring pastor reflects on his years of ministry with his congregation: "My first baptism, the boy grew up and became an atheist. My first confirmand, the girl backslid and left the faith. My first marriage ended up in divorce. But good news: My first funeral, the man stayed in the ground where I put him."

The peace of our Lord, Eric,
in holy detachment (kind of),

Dad

THE SIXTH LETTER

---

30 July 2000

Dear Eric,

Sunday afternoon, I think it's the Eighth Sunday after Pentecost, and your mother and I are relishing our Sabbath. She just completed letters to your children. I am rereading *The Source*—did you ever read it?[1] I've never particularly cared for Michener, never thought him a very good writer. But I am impressed by this—he has entered that entire Palestinian/Israeli/biblical world imaginatively and rendered it freshly.

We have had a pretty steady stream of guests the last couple of months, and the conversations have brought home details of what is going on in churches and among pastors. I really do believe that you are working in a very different world, working to develop a worshipping people who honor Jesus and one another as baptized brothers and sisters—a community of worship: both words, *community* and *worship*, at total odds with the culture as it is given to us.

Now that I am not in the thick of it day by day, one of the things that seems to me to make pastoral/ecclesial life so difficult is the pervasive consumerism that dominates our lives. We are introduced to and embrace a gospel that is defined by the Trinity—God in community, God in personal relationship: Father, Son, and Holy Spirit in constant and relentless relationship in the Godhead and with us. But we are trained from the cradle to be consumers. And a consumer is the epitome of passivity, of thingness. That sets the tone for virtually everything that goes on in society, including church life.

What happens, then, is that the gospel is packaged in such a way that consumers will buy it. It's the only way they know how to make choices, how to get on in life. And so we pastors, without even being aware of what we are doing, package the gospel—images, words, goals, visions, names, etc.—so that it will get people's attention and attract them. It is not that we are distorting the message itself, but we are presenting it in a way that people will want it.

But here's the problem: The gospel is essentially relational—personal to the core. It involves relationships and responses of the heart and assent of the will—all personal details. There is no single part of the gospel that can be presented or received impersonally. The Trinity is our most vigorous assertion of that. But packaging, by its very nature, obscures the personal. It provides a means that is not relational—it thingifies the persons of the Trinity—and also the person who is being addressed and invited.

The consequence is that it is possible, and very often happens, that we get people participating in the church, sometimes very enthusiastically and willingly, who are far more involved in the impersonal than in the personal. This is the difficulty with programs. Programs are necessary—it is simply not possible to deal with every person on his or her own, as a special case. If we are to do anything as a community, there have to be some programmatic guidelines and procedures and goals. But the program is essentially abstract and impersonal. It is possible to deal with people programmatically and avoid or obscure who they are, the uniquely personal. Not only possible, but far easier. Programs take far less time and energy than persons. Programs are far more efficient—persons require endless time and trouble (at least, enough of them do). And so the tendency, after a while, is to spend more time on the programs, where you get a lot more bang for the buck, than on persons.

Then, when you combine packaging with programming, you gradually erode the personal center of worship, of witness, of mission, of community itself. You end up with a crowd.

Now, here's what makes it even worse (or harder): The people we live with know what it's like to be sold packaged products and to be enlisted in programs. And they like it. It's easier than being a person in relationship. And so they come to a church that offers them the gospel as a product and the Christian life as a program, and they love it; they can have all the promises and blessings that the gospel is famous for without all the anxieties and doubts and struggles of faith. No wonder the product/program churches flourish—it is the gospel retooled for a consumer culture.

I'm convinced that there is no "answer" to this. This is the way the world is today—in some ways, it has always been this way, but previous generations usually labeled the challenge as idolatry—the depersonalization and manipulation of God. But with the culture so totally commodified, it is difficult to see this in spiritual or religious terms. And the continuities with the idolatry language of our Scriptures get more and more remote with each passing month.

And that means that pastors today need to be vigilant and discerning in an area that they didn't have to in earlier generations—a front that doesn't look like an enemy front. Because packaging and programming appear to be on our side, helping us do what we are already doing less effectively and competently. We hardly notice what is happening—the depersonalization that subtly but surely takes place.

The discernment requires a lot of savvy, for we can't just throw out the packaging and the programming the way we could throw out the heresies and the immoral behaviors classically associated with idolatries. We have to hunt and pick our way without clear guidelines. Which I think you are doing pretty well, but we can't be too careful.

These reflections were triggered when I learned that Joel and his family had joined your congregation. I remember our earlier conversation after the Sunday you put on your robe and stole and Joel's comment that he thought they were looking for "sacred space, and I think we have found it." I doubt whether Joel and his family would be in your congregation today, at least not in the way they are, without the kind of personal and detached (that is, not sales-oriented) attention with which you related to them.

I like the way you go about your work, Eric: slowly, patiently, not feeling rushed or panicked into extraordinary strategies that promise much—and certainly do "work" on the culture's terms.

I guess what we do is plug away, day by day, wary of the packaging and programming (but not able to function without them, either), constantly looking for ways to assert the personal—speaking names, avoiding, as much as possible, depersonalized forms of conversation, whether in choice of words or in methods of conveying the message. Refusing to let "efficiency" dictate the bottom line.

Words are important. I have, as you know, an aversion to labeling the place I work as an "office" and insist on "study." I never told other people what they should call it; I just referred to it that way myself: "Meet me in my study." "Call me at my study." If we go to the office every day, people expect us to do office work and we end up doing office work.

I have added a couple more words to my black list: *dysfunctional*—it is an impersonal word. Engines and machines are dysfunctional, but not people. People are not to be understood in terms of how or whether they function (the disabled, the mentally deficient, the elderly) but in terms of who they are, their relationships, and mostly, their relationship with God. The word seems harmless and vivid at first, but it works its way into our consciousness and ends up doing harm.

And *resource*—referring to people as resources. Again, an impersonal term that values a person primarily in terms of what we can get out of them or what they can offer us. The word obscures the essential core of soul identity. Not all at once, but after a generation or two of this, something happens to the way we view and treat people.

Those two words between them are at least partly responsible for the culture we live in now, which is so thoroughly functionalized and depersonalized. I don't think we can be too careful about our words.

And the words we use in worship are so critical, so influential, so basic to the formation of an imagination that is alive with relationship and responsiveness, a community of unique souls who are related to one another not by their tasks or their needs but by, in the long run, love—the most intimate and personal work of God in our lives and for us with each other.

Another detail that is more present before you than it was for me: You have a lot more people advising and urging and directing you to package the products and manage the resources and program the people than I ever did. You are simply battered with culture counsel. It's hard to tune out those voices, especially when at least half of what they say is true and useful. It's the mind-set, not the item-by-item stuff, that corrupts the pastoral/ecclesial mind and soul.

You are working, Eric, in what Isaiah calls (this in the
KJV) the "habitation of dragons."[2] Dangerous country.
You know how continually and solemnly I and your mom
pray for you and your family and congregation. You are
creating, or subcreating, a new community of persons
formed in Christ—*Christ*ians! But mostly what it feels like
is sheer plod.

We are anticipating your arrival in August.

With much proud love . . .

Dad

THE SEVENTH LETTER

—

19 October 2000

Dear Eric,

You've got me thinking and scratching my head with your request "to hear more about how you've come to understand and integrate the parts of who you are."

I don't think about it much anymore, although I once did. I also made lists of the sort you have. It's interesting, in hindsight, that running always was in my lists. I can't do that anymore. And I'm still the same person. Walking is what's left of that, and I'm grateful to be able to do that. My workshop was usually in my lists, but not as prominently as yours—I think that is a deeper piece of identity for you than me. The workshop, for me, is more a place to immerse myself in stuff—get my hands on something rather than make something, although some making does come out of it. (Remember your old toy box? I had it stripped of the paint, and I have just finished five coats of a clear finish that keeps the old look and feel of the forty-year-old pine boards and attached one of those hinges that gives the lid a slow descent—for Hans and Anna. Pleasant hours doing that.) You have such a magnificent workshop now—I quite agree that it is essential and as central to your identity as your study.

When I was thirty and we moved to Bel Air to start the church, I was pretty well formed as a Christian, felt at home in living the faith, had a pretty secure identity in my thinking and praying. Marriage with Jan seemed a gift, and I did feel mostly "put together." Up until then, everything had seemed to unfold quite naturally.

But being a pastor threw me into a tailspin. It really did. I think for the first time in my life, I was in over my head, didn't know what I was doing, and had no confidence. I felt that I had a basket of identity fragments—pieces of Pentecostalism and Presbyterianism, professor and writer pieces, gummed up with ill-defined anticlerical prejudices, plus a lot of other stuff that no longer fit together—and I was trying not to get rid of any of it because all the pieces were really *me*, but not knowing how to do it. Those were what Jan now calls the "blue funk" years.

I think that the first important thing that took place during those years was that I gave up thinking I was going to amount to anything. It took a while, because I had always assumed that I would get to the top of something or other. But it became clear that being a pastor in the Presbyterian church would not get me anywhere that I always thought I wanted to go—I wasn't good at, nor did I care about, what Presbyterian pastors considered important.

At the same time, I was sure I was where I was supposed to be. Odd, now, that I never doubted that. I had a deep sense that being in Bel Air and Presbyterian was God appointed. So there was no thought of changing or leaving or getting out. But I did have to reimagine my future in much more modest terms. This sounds a little overdramatic now, but it sure felt like it at the time: I settled down to be a failure. I hoped that I could be a faithful failure, and I hoped that I could keep a small congregation together while my pastoral identity was being formed out of all those fragments.

And it gradually was formed. All the while, I was learning to preach, learning to treat sinners as souls, learning the nature of institution, learning to write—but the formation took place, mainly, I think, because I wasn't trying to figure out how to "make it" as a Presbyterian or a new church developer. My new acceptance of the self-identity of "failure" freed me from much of the muck of programming and promotion and the need to be noticed.

Not entirely, of course. It was slow work—six or seven years of feeling dislocated, not fitting, incompetent. But the Scripture-prayer, prayer-Scripture mornings, plus your mother's affection and acceptance (and who knows how many other unnoticed people and things) gradually began to give shape to all those pieces without having to throw any of them out. By the time I was thirty-eight, I was feeling much like I did in my pre-pastor days, except now I was feeling it as a pastor.

One thing that in retrospect looms as a major element in the pastor-person formation was our trip to Montana each summer. This place held all (or nearly all) the details of identity together in their prefragmented state. Returning here annually provided a kind of base camp to catch my breath, to feel myself again, to pray through the identity stuff, to get in step again with the reality of my parents' world. Place is so identity affirming—at least it was that for me. And to have Jan and you children in these woods and mountains and lake—my world felt truly integrated, at least for that time. Then it was back again to the pastor-in-formation months. But that repeated rhythm of return to place now seems to me to be a major factor in keeping all the pieces of my life available for the pastor identity.

The element most conspicuously missing in all this is play. I've never integrated play easily and unselfconsciously into who I am. You and Lynn and your children do this so much better than Jan and I have managed to do it (and Jan is better than me). We now plan and prepare for play, but it is not natural—it is rarely spontaneous. And I think now it contributes a serious handicap to the life of prayer. I sometimes talk and write about the similarity between praying and playing—both are necessary, neither "makes anything happen," both are uncoerced and therefore totally free acts. I'm convinced, but I'm still learning.

Is that what you asked for? The formation/integration of the parts of my life, as I look over what I have written, mostly came about through those years of accepting a "failure identity," and every summer repeating the 2,500-mile return to this place. It doesn't look like I *did* much of anything except continue to go about my work, trying to be responsive to the Spirit's work.

I like the way you are making that place of yours so much yours—building and cultivating and tree-cutting and playing. How formative that is for both you and Lynn, but also for your children.

We are leaving in an hour or so for Seattle—SPU and the Image Conference, where I'll preach on Sunday.[1] We're staying at the downtown Hampton.

I love you,

Dad

THE EIGHTH LETTER

―

24 January 2001

Dear Eric,

I have been ruminating on my next Eric Letter
all month—and then yours came a few days ago, and
everything came into focus. Because I have been
thinking, praying a lot about your launch into the
building operations and remembering my own venture
into that unknown world. Here's what I remember . . .

Even though I didn't have any great enthusiasm for
building as such, I realized that if I didn't embrace
it as integral to my pastoral vocation, it would be a
waste. And so I pretty much deliberately moved from a
reluctant "I've just got to get through this" attitude to
an energetic embrace of all the details. In looking back

now, I think that the building and architectural details of those early years were an important element in the spiritual formation of the congregation, rooting it in place and stuff and materiality—all aspects of incarnation. And also my pastoral formation—keeping me physical and *there*, not separating the spiritual and the material or the spiritual and the secular (contractors, inspectors, workers on the job who always got very quiet when I showed up, which led me to think there had been some pretty heavy cussing going on). Here are some of the elements that, in retrospect, seem important.

Everything got formed in my own imagination, to begin with, in preaching and worship. I found great stories and texts in Haggai, Zechariah, Ezra, Nehemiah, and the last half of Exodus. I saturated myself in them, getting a feel for the tremendous emphasis that is given in our scriptural tradition to things and craft—a *place* of worship. That helped me, I think, to kindly and gently resist the desire of others to reproduce something out of their past—nostalgia architecture and worship.

I have just now finished translating Ezra and Nehemiah and gone over the edits for Exodus, and I realize how deeply those texts got embedded in my imagination through those building years. And I'm grateful for that now—all the stuff that was involved in the building, instead of being an interruption, became a

part of my pastoral vocation. I've sensed the same thing
going on with you, and that has pleased me a lot.

Another element in this that got formed in those
times was lay leadership. We didn't have any great,
natural leaders in our congregation; the new church-
development guy in the presbytery pushed me to depend
on professionals. But that didn't seem right to me, so
I resisted (with considerable fear and trembling) that
counsel and worked with what I had. We had an architect,
of course (Gerry Baxter), but he had never done a church
before. Russ Walls became the building chairperson;
he had no experience in this kind of thing either. But
Russ turned out to be perfect for the task: He shared the
leadership with others and was steady and reliable and
wise. By not being a conspicuously "strong" leader, there
was space for everyone else to be part of it. By the time
that first building phase was done, I think a style of lay
leadership had been formed that continued ever after. I
don't think I had a clear idea of what I was doing on this
front, but my initial instincts, I think, were right and
confirmed in many ways through the years following.

After that first building phase, we had two
others, one in the early seventies (Charlie Reiher was
chairperson), and the other in 1986/1987, right after we
returned from our sabbatical year (Stan Mitchell was
chairperson). That completed the master plan that we

had worked out at the beginning. In those final two building operations, I did much less than in the first one. There just didn't seem any need for me to do much; the lay leadership was both competent and confident. It did give me considerable pleasure to see the leadership go ahead so easily; I can't even remember attending a committee meeting in the third phase, but I must have somewhere along the line.

A few years later, we were just getting ready to leave for Pittsburgh. Russ and Charlie and Stan with their spouses all happened to be in Florida on vacation and got together; around dinner, they realized that together they had, over a period of twenty-two years, given the leadership that had resulted in the completed work. A kind of reunion for them.

One of the disappointing things in relation to the building was what happened after that first phase, when the sanctuary and small education building were completed. I was feeling really good about how integrated everything was—the worship and preaching and lay development and slow growth of the congregation—that this building was a way to give shape to time and space so as to serve worship and mission. Naively, I thought everyone was with me; they were so enthusiastic and "on board." And then the building was completed; we had a service of dedication. In about

three weeks, worship attendance began to slack off; each
Sunday, there were fewer people. When I would visit
people in their homes, they would say things like, "We
sure did it, didn't we!" "Wasn't that great how we pulled
that off!" Slowly, I realized that the adrenaline produced
by everything connected with the building wasn't what
I thought it was, namely, the Holy Spirit. I went to my
presbytery exec and told him what was happening, and
he said, "Start another building program—that's the
only thing that gets those people excited." I decided
that wasn't a good idea—I didn't want to develop a
congregation that substituted adrenaline for the Holy
Spirit. It was at least a year before we worked ourselves
back to the worship attendance that preceded our
building completion.

But in looking back, I don't know that I would have
done anything differently. I was getting all that stuff
integrated within me, and maybe that was enough—I had
years ahead still to get them in on it. And many did get
in on it, slowly, slowly.

I am very glad that I got to do the building programs.
The demands that a building program puts on pastoral
identity are very formative. They can, of course, destroy
you by turning you into a subcontractor or cheerleader
or whatever. But they can also be catalytic for fusing
the various social, community, worship, and vocational

energies into something coherent. Until writing this to you right now, I don't think I ever realized how influential those building operations were in keeping my pastoral vocation in touch with a whole world of energies and necessities that weren't natural to me—and getting them inside me.

One of my decisions during those times was to make sure that I was giving more than adequate attention to the people who weren't "good at anything." Who didn't have the ability or energy or even the interest in what others were excited about. I visited and called them more often than the others, trying to keep in step with the slowest ones, the stragglers. I didn't want anyone left out, and I don't think anyone was.

And I'm really glad that you are getting to do it too. You are already, and have been, doing the essential thing: keeping worship at the center of what you are doing, the prayers and preaching and praise. I love the easy pace in which you are going about it—I don't sense anything is being rushed or pushed through.

You ask if there are better ways to focus the congregation's energy. I think you are doing it right: keeping the worship and community/congregational relationships primary. The only serious mistake I think you can make is to let the building operations drive the congregation (instead of worship). But I don't sense any of that in what you write or say—the building stuff seems to be assimilated into something larger and more comprehensive; but neither is it held at a distance as something beneath or below the higher concerns of a really "spiritual" people.

But thanks for letting me in on it this way, giving me a chance to reflect on my long-ago working through these matters that you are doing freshly and in your own unique way. I feel like I am a member of your building committee!

Leif/Amy and company and Amy's folks are coming for dinner tonight; they are here for a week or so visiting.

You must be gearing up for your Guatemala trip; Jan and I are praying that that will be deepening and broadening both.

I love what you are doing, but even more *you*.

The peace of our Lord,

Dad

THE NINTH LETTER

—

7 April 2001

Dear Eric,

I anticipate that you are either home or just getting home from your Seattle holiday. I hope the change was refreshing. And now Holy Week.

I've been working for the last three months on my spring lectures (May) for Regent, and in the process, I have been carrying on an internal conversation with you. My title is *Practice Resurrection* (from a Wendell Berry poem),[1] and my topic is spiritual formation, in which I am trying to give some biblical rootage in the reality of the Resurrection.

But as I am doing this, I also keep wondering: Why aren't pastors very much interested in this, or among

those who are interested, why does it become a specialty?
You don't do this, I know—this seems entirely integrated
in the way you go about things; that's why you are so
congenial a partner in this conversation. Do you feel this
way about many of your colleagues? Spiritual formation
is the ground where we work, or at least, where pastoral
vocation has its broadest and deepest roots. But it seems
to be commonly passed over lightly by many, while a few
come along and embrace it as the latest thing.

I guess I've always (or nearly always) felt that spiritual
formation (or "soul formation," or "practicing the
Christian life") is simply what pastors do without calling
a lot of attention to it. And when undue attention is
called to it, it is somehow distorted or falsified. It is
the obvious thing that everybody expects us to do, that
without which we wouldn't be pastors: truckers drive
trucks, farmers plant crops, dentists fix teeth, pastors
work with souls-in-formation. But talking about it too
much or in the wrong context somehow gets in the way
of actually doing it.

A lot of people expect their pastors to do this,
but when they find that we don't, they revise their
expectations and get along with what's there. And when
the time comes that they want some extra help with their
souls, they go to the self-help books in the book stands
or pick up a magazine that—along with articles on how to

improve your sex life—also have something about cancer and prayer or meditation and golf. I just don't think most people think of pastors primarily as concerned with the spiritual formation of their lives.

And do you agree that pastors don't commonly have this self-understanding? (You and me excepted!) The Pentecostal pastors I grew up with certainly didn't; what they were mostly interested in was giving people a kick-start toward some new form of ecstasy—adrenaline confused with the Holy Spirit, or maybe the Holy Spirit confused with adrenaline. And my life among the Presbyterians, while different and more congenial, hasn't been much of an improvement in this department—spiritual formation is, for the most part, given a back seat to satisfying the congregation's self-diagnosed needs.

It always strikes me as odd that when someone shows up who is just doing the ordinary, everyday work of pastor, he or she stands out like a sore thumb and gets labeled with something dismissive: maverick or crank or (and this is *really* dismissive) "mystic" or "saint."

Why is this? You are not supposed to answer these questions—unless, of course, you have the answers. But every once in a while, I get hit by this massive sense of isolation, a kind of vocational loneliness that seems out of proportion to the actual circumstances of my life. For instance, I have a pastor here, W____, who does it right, and I have you, already way ahead of me in this business. And I pick up an occasional friend along the way who has similar instincts and doesn't mind admitting it. Why isn't that enough?

By the way, I found a new writer that I think you would appreciate. Not a pastor, unfortunately, but close— an undertaker. Thomas Lynch. He knows a thing or two about spiritual formation. He writes about his work and knows something about souls. I have two of his books: *The Undertaking: Life Studies from the Dismal Trade,*[2] and *Bodies in Motion and at Rest: On Metaphor and Mortality.*[3] A friend put me on to these. They might be in the library, as they were both well-reviewed a couple of years ago. Lynch also writes poetry, but I haven't read any of that.

Anyway, back to spiritual formation and wondering why pastors aren't more attentive and at ease in this world. As I have been working through the canonical Resurrection stories, I am struck in a fresh way how noncompelling the Resurrection appearances were. Recognition seemed to come gradually for some and involved some readiness and responsiveness for it to "take." All the appearances were in the context of personal relationships and engagement—no public demonstrations. Paul took up the Resurrection and used it for apologetic purposes, but the Gospel writers seem to me to be not interested in that but in giving us stories

of the way it is when we find ourselves in the company
of the risen Christ. One of the things that is noticeable
from a pastoral stance is that there doesn't seem to be
any dramatic improvement in those first participants.
"Some doubted," seven disciples went back to fishing, and
Cleopas and friend, who must have been familiar with
Jesus in person, didn't have a clue in that three-hour walk
to Emmaus with him.[4] The disciples in the locked room
already had hard evidence from Mary of the Resurrection,
and they were still confused and afraid. Etc., etc.

I guess all I am trying to assimilate and get a detailed
feel for is that spiritual formation is a long and complex
process, not simple or quick. It started out this way,
and it's not going to ever be any different. There is no
template to be imposed on each person to diagnose what
needs improving and no "tests" to evaluate progress or
maturity.

But for people who expect to be able to evaluate and
measure and "get something out of it," this is not easy to
comprehend. And so it is hard for pastors to be content
with this low-profile existence when expectations are
so otherwise. I know that for me, this tension between
wanting to please my parishioners and wanting to truly
tend to their soul formation was constant and never went
away. I kept thinking there was a "solution" to it, but I
never found it; I just had to keep working in the tension.

When I get these lectures completed and delivered, you'll see how much of you there is in them, so much of what you are doing and things you've said—how pervasive this internal conversation has been for the last months, and what is now coming of it.

I'm thinking of myself these days as your associate pastor—do you have money in the budget for me?

With much love,
Dad

THE TENTH LETTER

—

25 September 2001

Dear Eric,

It's been a while since the last Eric Letter, but I've been pregnant for a while and am ready to deliver (it hasn't been quite nine months!). And September 11 uncovers my text. I know that you have been dealing with all this nonstop with your congregation and family; the big difference compared to me is that I haven't had a congregation to tend to, and I realize how different that is. When I was with my congregation, I'm not sure I ever felt the full impact of disaster—I was always tending to *them* in their experience of disaster, praying and searching the Scriptures and being with them. While I was certainly affected, there was always a feeling of intimacy present in the suffering—I was doing something in which the Holy Spirit was active, which gave some sense of meaning, even if I couldn't articulate it (which I mostly couldn't). In the most mundane sense, I had something to do, which I liked doing and was good at, if nothing more than sharing in helplessness, which meant that I wasn't as helpless as the people I was with.

But world events and catastrophe, because they were separated from present circumstances, were the least congenial areas of my pastoral life. Which is odd, because they are certainly prominent in Scripture. But as I have thought about it, there are a couple of things that I wonder about.

One, when disaster intervened in the congregation, there was a certain sense that I was the one giving solace, being there, praying, giving salvation perspective. And even though other people were involved, my position had a certain dignity and authority to it. These people were already involved in a network of worship and prayer; I would have been in their homes and played softball with them at the church picnic, etc. But with national disaster, my voice is drowned out by the media, the politicians, the editorial comments, and (in the case of September 11) an enormous amount of verbalized hate and fear from subgroups and subcultures. I don't have my congregation to myself. My voice, which seems personal and present in local and congregational disasters, now seems remote and just another opinion when the stage becomes worldwide.

The only comparable events to September 11 that I had to deal with pastorally were the assassinations of President Kennedy and Martin Luther King, and in a much less dramatic way, the Gulf War. I can still remember (I was younger then than you are now) how incompetent and at loose ends I felt. The authority I usually experienced in opening the Scriptures in the pulpit was now upstaged by TV commentators and politicians and the newspapers, to say nothing of the louder opinion-makers in the neighborhood.

The other thing I wonder about regarding my own sense of now knowing what I am doing in relation to the Big Bad Things is my conviction that pastoral work has mostly to do with obedience right here, in the cultivation of love in the circumstances of family and neighborhood and workplace, to searching the Scriptures as a text for living in the details of the here and now. The big things—heaven and hell, death and judgment—are all matters of the politics of the Kingdom of God that we pray will come both daily and finally and presently strive to live according to its conditions and promises and covenants. But I'm never sure about how the Kingdom of America fits into it—or maybe more to the point, I am wary of equating the two, and so when all the "God Bless America" rhetoric heats up, I feel very much an outsider in the culture and yet hesitant to say anything, lest I be judged as unpatriotic or even seditious.

I wrote *Where Your Treasure Is* (having preached and taught it first) trying to get that all figured out. I learned a lot in the process, but I still don't ever feel that I assimilated it into my pastoral intuitions and practices.

And so that is the way I am feeling these days as I imagine you in your pastoral work, dealing with something far beyond what I ever had to do in relation to our nation and culture. So I pray for you daily in this testing and deepening of your pastor life, but I don't have any wisdom, as you provide your congregation with images and promises and commands that hopefully make their participation in the politics of the Kingdom something deeper and more lasting than their responses and feelings and opinions that are evoked by the terror of the present.

We're leaving for Vancouver tomorrow. Will take two days to drive. I am giving lectures on Genesis 1 and 2, "The Gift of Time" and "The Gift of Place"[1] for the evangelical conservationist group called A Roche (have we talked about it?). We'll be there Friday and Saturday, leave Saturday afternoon, and get to your place sometime on Sunday afternoon for an overnight. We'll be calling you to check if that is still okay.

I'm getting down to the wire on *The Message*. Just a little editing left—two or three more weeks.

Much love,

Dad

THE ELEVENTH LETTER

—

11 November 2001

Dear Eric,

We took a few days away for a birthday celebration.
Left Wednesday for the Izaak Walton Inn and stayed
two nights. An old railroad inn, full of railway nostalgia.
Hiked some new trails across the Middle Fork into
Glacier Park. On Friday we drove east to Fort Benton,
on the Missouri. I've never been there and wanted to
fulfill an old curiosity. It was a great visit. I had no idea
it was such a central place in the history of Montana. So
we came back last night full of new stories and legends
and lore about our state.

On the long drive back (five hours), I started plotting
my next Eric Letter. I realized that what is working its

way in my imagination these days is the trivialization
that is going on in pastoral vocations and in the church.
I think what started this off was a memorial service in
the Kalispell Presbyterian Church three weeks ago. Chet
Ellingson died at eighty-one, after a miserable two-year
illness. Geri, his widow (I don't know how much you
remember of the family), asked her pastor if I could
participate in the service, and he generously invited me.
I know the pastor slightly—we have had lunch together a
couple of times. He was more than generous, actually—he
virtually turned the whole service over to me. And I was
grateful, for Chet was one of the formative people in my
adolescent years. It was a good service, and I was very
glad to be part of it.

But what got under my skin was being around the
pastor. His office (definitely not a study) was full of
trivia—cartoons and posters and assorted junk. And our
conversation before and after the service was the kind
you do between innings at a baseball game. The two
lunches I had had with him in the past year were the
same—church is pretty much a matter of dealing with
problems and developing strategies and gossiping about
politics. And since then, I have realized how common
this is, how pervasive it is in our church/pastor culture.

I had hoped in a vague kind of way that September
11 would do away with all that; that the realization

of the seriousness of our vocation would wipe out all
the silliness; that the apocalyptic dimensions of the
everydayness of our times would convince every pastor in
the country that so much hangs on our taking each soul
with a terrible and holy seriousness. I don't mean, as you
know, that we are solemn—laughter and leisure are also
involved in holy seriousness—but that the centrality of
our calling as expressed in the way we conduct worship
and the way we treat these baptized souls around us is
critical to the way the Kingdom comes.

I observe the way that you go about your work. And
do I ever appreciate it. The way you maintain that clear
gospel focus, the detached way you conduct your life
by caring for people without becoming managerial with
them, obsessed with getting them "in line." The way
you keep your children primary and attended to in all
their individualities. The way you have given careful
theological and liturgical attention to your church
architecture, and the process of building itself.

But back to our pastoral vocation. I had thought that
I was done writing about the pastoral life. And now that
The Message is done (or just about), that I would go on to
my spiritual-theology books. And I guess I will, but I
wonder if there is anything to do about calling attention
to the way church life is conducted these days. And the
thoughtless ways in which pastors so uncritically accept

it and go along with it. We are living in apocalypse, and pastors don't notice.

Which means that the spiritual lives of our parishioners are left to the care of journalists and politicians. There is nothing wrong with them as such— they have their jobs to do and are doing them according to their rights. But never before in my lifetime (World War II with the Holocaust and the atomic bombs was comparable, I suppose, but I was too young to know it) has the apocalyptic substratum of everyday reality been so evident. And instead of pastors entering their pulpits and nursing homes and hospitals with an imagination steeped in the visions and poetry of the prophets, we get variations on "God Bless America" religion from one sector and angry denunciations and invective from another. Meanwhile, the ordinary Christians in our churches get no hint that this is the exact kind of world in which the gospel was formed and continues to provide adequate resources for living in hope and love.

Our own pastor, W____, whom I respect immensely, and who could never be accused of being superficial or silly, still has absolutely no sensitivity to what is going on in his parishioners' lives right now. Since the first Sunday after September 11, he has not mentioned even one time the world conditions which dominate the imaginations of most of his congregation. Not

once. It is as if nothing in the newspaper or on
television requires any reorientation in the world of
the gospel and the Kingdom of God. We have parents
and grandparents in our congregation whose kids and
grandkids have been mobilized and sent off with their
reserve units. Not a word in the prayers.

There is one way to interpret this that is positive—
that the Kingdom is so much more present and real
that we don't need to even give the world the time of
day or a nod of recognition. But I'm not sure that that
is very pastoral. Maybe the terrorists as such don't
require that much gospel attention, but terrorized souls
certainly do.

And I certainly don't think that the pastoral task is
to create a stampede to give the impression that we are
DOING SOMETHING. Or exploit emotions in order
to push an agenda.

I don't want to end up just being cranky about all this.
But I do long and pray for the development of a pastoral
mind and spirit that seriously, patiently, and cheerfully
engages this mix of souls and Scriptures that makes up the
congregations of our land.

Anyway, just consider this a conversation, not a
pronouncement. I'm sure that there are a lot of pastors
doing something along these lines—you can't be the
only one!

Your mother and I are looking forward to Thanksgiving and the joy of celebration and the goodness of family.

With much love,

Dad

THE TWELFTH LETTER

———

26 January 2002

Dear Eric,

Do you remember Norval Hegland—the skinny
Norwegian pastor (retired) who loved flying airplanes?
He died last week, at eighty-six years. In the last few
weeks of his life, when it was clear that he was dying, I
visited him several times. Those last weeks he had his
daughters, Mary and Ruth, and his niece Marilyn with
him—not all at once, but always at least one of them. His
wife, Margaret, died several months ago. He was too
weak to talk much, but the visits were as good as they
could be. I feel very honored and privileged to have been
in on such a good death—not only for him, but for the
daughters and niece too. He died at home as he wanted

to do, full of appreciation for his pastoral life. And for me, being in his company during the weeks of his dying, there was a lot of reflective appreciation on being given this pastoral way of life (although I hope there are a few more years left to it!).

The funeral was simply magnificent. It's the tradition among the Montana Lutherans (I don't know if it extends beyond here) when a pastor dies for all available pastors to vest, sit together, and sing an anthem. There were about twelve or fourteen present, all vested in their white robes, filling three or four pews at the front left. (W____ invited me, but I didn't really feel part of the "club" and so excused myself.) They processed in and took their places. At the appointed time, they assembled in the chancel and sang a hymn from the hymnbook— unrehearsed, I suspect, but tolerable. But it was so moving to have those pastors give this witness and tribute to a colleague pastor. Norval's children each spoke, wonderful tributes to his years as father and husband and pastor. As the stories accumulated, it became evident that he had lived his entire life on the margins—in tiny churches in North Dakota and Montana, and for many years in Alaska flying his airplane from parish to parish, with special concern for the Eskimos, founding a church in Nome for them. And all the time advocating social- and economic-justice concerns (many sharply

worded letters to politicians and others), maintaining
serious biblical and theological studies, and flying and
maintaining his airplanes (I hadn't known that he was a
skilled mechanic). And then W____ uncorked one of his
best sermons. W____, as you know, always does serious,
solid work in the pulpit, but it is often wooden, doctrinal,
what your mother calls "so Lutheran," with little
imagination or relationship. But every once in a while,
he launches a masterpiece, and this was one of them:
personal, simple, gospel, accurate, totally illuminating
both text and occasion.

The experience—the visiting and the service itself—
is still reverberating in me. It is so reassuring and
confirming to know that the pastoral life can still be
lived with such integrity and honor, and it fills me with
continuing gratitude that I got in on living this unique
life of serving God in this way.

It bothers me a lot when some of my former students
go for glitzy career positions in the big-business
churches. This happened several times in the last couple
of years—maybe that is why Norval—the evidence of such
a thoroughly unselfconscious and Christ-serving pastoral
life—has meant so much to me. A confirmation that it can
still happen.

I finished preparing the sermon for the dedication
of Colbert Presbyterian a few days ago. I knew I was

going to have to get a good head start on it. It is so hard for me to prepare sermons now, when I am not involved in the day-by-day life of the congregation. I look back now and wonder how I did it every week for thirty-plus years. When I'm not living with, praying with and for, alternately getting mad at and celebrating the congregation, nothing connects. But I finally succeeded in cobbling something together with prayer and baling wire that I hope won't embarrass you.

There's a lot more to it than that, as I'm sure you know. I am so pleased that you asked me to be part of this celebration/dedication of your Genesis Center, giving physical witness to the incarnated gospel being worked out and developed on those several hundred square feet of Washington soil. And to be there, on site, as these years of your own pastoral life get expressed in a form and place so saturated with prayer and Scripture and personal relationships. I would have been happy to have just taken up the offering, but preparing the sermon has forced me to think through again just what it is that you and the congregation have done.

Your mom and I spent yesterday morning preparing chicken cacciatore in anticipation of a friend from Calgary (Joyce Peasgood, my TA at Regent) coming to visit for a couple of days. But she just called saying she couldn't come. It is twenty-six degrees below zero in

Calgary with snow accumulating by the hour—a classic prairie blizzard. So here we are with this magnificent meal and no one to eat it. We'll have to go out to the highways and byways and compel them to come in, I guess.

With much love,

Dad

THE THIRTEENTH LETTER

—

15 April 2002

Dear Eric,

I know Mother told you that we went out Saturday
and dug up eight ponderosa seedlings and planted them
here. All the time we were doing it, I kept remembering
when you helped Matt Matthews plant all those white
pines around the borders of Christ Our King. I like
thinking about that; it seems such a complete metaphor
for church building, family building, community
building, a building that is not hammering something
together but placing something in the ground that all
heaven and earth makes grow—but slowly, slowly, slowly.

And now I am watching Tony from across the bay
change his waterfront with brute force. A few days ago,

huge trucks started coming in and dumping huge boulders on the side of the hill—I mean huge: boulders six feet in diameter. We had no idea what he was doing. And then a couple of days later, two more machines, a large front-end loader and a tractor with a claw shovel on a beam (I don't know what they are called), started moving the boulders to the edge of the precipice down to the lake, rolling them down and then building a retaining rock wall fifteen feet or so out into the lake, filling it in, making a patio between his two docks. Today another engine arrived and shot gravel the sixty feet from the top of the hill down into the retaining wall, filling it and leveling it off. For several days now, we have been assaulted by noise and watched this violence against the land as Tony imposes his will on this piece of creation that he holds title to. The expense has to be enormous—$15,000 or $20,000, I would think. And why? He is rarely here. He is never outside when he is here, except to take his boat out occasionally. Apparently, he has this lust to make something happen, prove he is in control, make his presence known/felt. Show the earth and the world who is boss around here.

The two building operations seem parabolic—two ways of dealing with place and people, entering into what is there and planting seeds and waiting for the life to mature, or hauling in machines and impatiently rearranging soil and rock to assert control and mastery.

The way of you and Matt thirty years ago, and the way of Tony this week. And the way you have developed your congregation, slowly, prayerfully, attentively, and respectfully of the people whom you were given, in contrast to so much of the current Promethean, depersonalized church methods.

I have been thinking about this these days because I am preparing to speak to the Rocky Mountain Wee Kirk Conference at the end of this month in Colorado Springs (it was originally scheduled for Jackson Hole; I don't know why it was changed). They assigned me texts from 1 John, and so I have been immersing myself there. One of the things that I am so much impressed with in John's approach to his congregation is that he treats them with so much dignity, so much respect. He could have been condescending because they should have known better than to end up in the kind of squabbles that must have been going on (reading between the lines). But he never wavers from intimate language, from relational concern— even when he is taking a severe line with them.

And I don't know why this is so rare among church leaders. The church becomes a cause or a project or a "vision" and gets abstracted into a generalization so that relationships (and, of course, the love that is John's primary concern) are marginalized and diluted into bromides.

But here's a story that sounds a better note. I don't know if we have mentioned Bob and Amy Jones to you. Bob is pastor of a Baptist church in Cranbrook (Canada). They have done good work and are much appreciated. He has been there twelve years; a year ago, he began getting depressed and at the end of his rope and came down here a few times to talk it over. Jan and I suggested a sabbatical; the church agreed to it. They took six months at Schloss Mittersill in Austria, which we financed. They came back refreshed but also with no enthusiasm for doing church business as usual—the Baptists are very big on programs and promotion. Bob confessed his lack of interest in meeting their expectations and said maybe he should prepare to leave. They called in the regional church official, the "bishop," who met with their church leaders and Bob, got a feel for the lay of the land, heard them affirm that Bob was the best pastor, preacher, teacher they had ever had but that they really felt they needed someone who would put them on the map and make the programs go. The "bishop" agreed that they had to have somebody who would take charge. So Bob and Amy came down here three weeks ago and talked over the whole thing again. It became clear that Bob really loved being pastor to these people. And if he left, he had no heart to go to another church that wanted him to "run the church." We talked on the phone a week or so ago, and I lamented that the "bishop" was ready to sacrifice one of his best pastors to the congregation's desire for some more enthusiastic programs. We just got a card from them yesterday: Amy wrote that the leaders had met the evening before and realized that Bob might really leave, and who would they get in his place? In their discussion, they decided that maybe they really didn't want a "religious" church, but perhaps something along the lines that Bob and Amy have been doing with them for twelve years now, which is relational and pastoral, with a focus on preaching and teaching and being with them in their homes and work.

The story isn't over yet, but to tell you the truth, I could hardly believe what we read on that postcard—Jan read it to me driving into town.

Anyway, that's what I've been thinking about these days, grateful that you know how to treat a congregation with the dignity of "children of God . . . and who knows what we shall be," planting seeds and hanging around long enough to see them grow.[1] Sequoias?

Much love to you, Eric,
with continuing prayers as you love those people.

THE FOURTEENTH LETTER

—

29 October/19 November 2002

Dear Eric,

I don't know why I'm having such a hard time getting
focused on this letter to you. I started nearly three weeks
ago, and I keep pressing the delete button. So here I go
again. Let me start with what happened earlier this week,
the trip I mentioned on the telephone.

I went to Tyler, Texas, on Tuesday and came back on
Wednesday. This is the first time I have done anything
in the way of promotion of *The Message*. The publicist
at NavPress prevailed on me several months ago, said
she thought this was really important. She was wrong. I
was in the wrong country with the wrong people. The
occasion was a breakfast for pastors that a chain of

bookstores does every year. They had two hundred-plus pastors, and they had me talk about *The Message*. Which I did. They were all very appreciative and gracious, so I should be grateful. But they were also full of clichés and self-satisfaction at being in such a Christian town and state, with such a Christian president presiding over the world just now. After all these years, I realize that I have never been immersed in such a total Bible Belt world. All the glossy women looked the same; all the pastors sounded the same. The bookstore that the manager was so proud of was very large, with extensive holdings of every kind of CD, tape, and music publication, vast displays of Christian-romance fiction, a huge gallery of Thomas Kinkade. I had mentioned Wendell Berry in my address to the pastors. They had never heard of him. There was not a single book in the store that was not certified Southern evangelical.

Why am I so uncomfortable in this world? They are all on my side; they are all courteous and affirmative, but it seems to be a gospel without depth, without suffering, without ambiguity. Everything smoothed out and ironed, and with a lot of starch in the collar. Why don't I ever fit?

And now that I write this, I think maybe this is why I have had trouble getting into the stride of this letter. For several months now, since the NavPress celebration party, I have spent more time with "evangelicals" than I am used to, and the effects are beginning to accumulate. I am used to a wider range of emotion and more forthrightness in matters of doubt and despair. It feels as if the people who are saying *Amen* to what I have been doing are doing it more as a celebrity thing than out of their own lives—the applause seems a little canned.

I'm feeling a little better already, just noticing all this.

And here is a reflection that has been growing in the process. The main work of the church in our culture, I am beginning to feel, has to do with "ways and means." When everybody knows the gospel and is happy to be saved (and that is just the extreme instance of what is pretty common in so many church circles), the thing that stands out negatively is the inappropriateness of their ways and means: All their admiration is for the big and the glamorous, the image and the numbers. The most significant thing about *The Message*—to judge from their comments—is that it has sold seven million copies. I'm not sure what the Senate Ways and Means Committee does, but my feeling is that it is one of the more influential committees in the Senate. Do we have an equivalent of such a thing among us?

I'm beginning to think (or maybe it's what I have thought all along) that this is what pastors are primarily responsible for: the ways and means by which we guide people into obedience and trust. In a technologically obsessed culture, our imaginations are quite naturally dominated by ways and means. Since all technology is by definition good, there is no critical attention or discernment available—anything that looks good and makes people feel good and gets a lot of good people together must be good.

The devil's three temptations of Jesus all had to do with ways and means. Every one of the devil's goals was excellent. The devil had an unsurpassed vision statement. But the ways and means were incompatible with the ends. Jesus saw through it at once; why are pastors so intoxicated with visions and goals and so muddled when it comes to ways and means?

The difficulty is that concern for ways and means, which is the heart of the contemplative life, is very low on the agenda of the American pastor, especially for the pastor who wants to make an "impact" on the culture. Even the word *contemplative* itself is consigned to the far margins of interest, something to be indulged occasionally, perhaps on a weekend retreat or on a walk through the woods.

When I am in Tyler, Texas, and its many suburbs that fill the pews in evangelical congregations all over the country, I am simply overwhelmed with the seeming impossibility of arousing any interest in caring about ways and means—how we live this life the way Jesus led us to do it. The ways and means adopted by all my erstwhile and admiring friends revolve around instant communication, efficiency, hurry, planning, and counting. Anything small or slow, which includes any person small or slow, is treated with condescension.

Your mother and I have been thinking about this trust—we have named it the Selah Trust—and so have been trying to get a focus on just what it is that we have been about all our lives and how we want our money to be used in a way consistent with that. The word that keeps coming up is *contemplation*. What we are looking for is not primarily the causes and ends that people / organizations are committed to, but how they go about it—the test for gospel authenticity is the *way*, not the *what*.

Standard fundraising is all about the what. Any *how* will do, so long as it brings in the money. So we find ourselves staying very local, very close to the ground, as we make our decisions and plans.

I am not sure, Eric, that this is a letter; it qualifies more as a rant.

At one time in the course of those earlier deletions, I started out by reflecting on what it feels like to be seventy. But that will come later. Actually, it feels pretty good. I can't remember being as reflective regarding any other decade marker. There is a contemplative feel to this one. But maybe I had to get the "rant" out of my system to get down to what is really going on in me.

With much love,

Dad

THE FIFTEENTH LETTER

―

25 January 2003

Dear Eric,

Since Thanksgiving I've been carrying with me an image that it's time to share with you. Do you remember the way Virgil's *Aeneid* opens? (I think it is the opening— I don't have a copy here). The Trojans have been defeated by the Greeks, and Aeneas, one of the Trojans, is escaping from the city. He is on his way, embarked on his life's work, a journey that will eventually result in founding the city of Rome. His father, Anchises, is too old to make the journey, but Aeneas refuses to leave him behind, even though it is going to slow him down considerably. So as he leaves Troy, he has his old dad, Anchises, draped over his shoulders, unwilling to abandon his origins in order to do something new, "on his own," so carrying him with him at considerable inconvenience.

The triggering moment for this image at Thanksgiving was when you and I went down to the lake to take out the kayaks for a paddle. You picked up the kayaks effortlessly. I was stiff and awkward getting in. You unobtrusively helped me to get launched without a mishap. And then we were off. That's when I first realized the juxtaposition of our birthdays: your approaching fortieth and my just past seventieth, your limber strength and my diminished agility, you stroking the kayak powerfully and swiftly, me still part of the journey, but lagging, with diminished strength. And while out on the lake that day, the image came: I saw myself as Anchises draped across your shoulders.

I didn't say anything at the time. I *couldn't* say anything at the time. The realization was too fresh—I needed to ponder it, to meditate on the implications, to let the memories surface and connect. But I can say it now: Happy birthday, Eric.

Birthdays never meant much to me, as I'm sure you've noticed. My parents never made much of them. In fact, I don't remember Karen or Ken or me ever having a birthday party or cake. I don't think there was any lack of love in evidence, it was just that the Lord was returning soon, and we didn't have time for such frivolities. Your mother has tried hard to compensate for my "birthday-challenged" psyche, but I limp while she dances.

But this one is different. As I reflect and pray now in and around your fortieth birthday, you and your family and your work seem so healthy, so biblically holy. Much of what I'm feeling is probably just selfish—what *I* am getting out of it. But it feels like you are completing and confirming so much of what your mom and I were setting out to do forty years ago—but now, forty years later, you're doing it better, more relaxed, more confident. I spent all those years trying to learn how to be a pastor, and then you just up and did it. Your pastoral and family life are so integrated.

Jan and I were at an environmental meeting a few weeks ago to hear the writer Terry Tempest Williams speak. She was introduced by Rick Bass, a local writer who lives up in the Yaak. Do you know the name, the writing? Leif likes him a lot. Anyway, he introduced her. Rick is a superb writer but also a very active advocate for the wilderness, working hard for environmental causes and therefore in perpetual opposition to logging/mining interests in his area. I had never seen him before. He is forty-five or fifty, rather small of stature, elf-like—cheerful and light. The thing that was impressive about

him was his fierce advocacy of matters environmental
combined with a complete absence of "fight"—no
bitterness, cynicism, accusation, rancor, anger. None. I
started making associations between him and the family
and pastoral lives that you and I live. And then I came
across an essay that he had written on glaciers. I have
copied it out and am sending it to you. But it is Saturday
today and the PO isn't open, and I need to have it
weighed for postage. So I am going to send this letter
now and the larger envelope on Monday. You might
still not get it for your birthday, but I want this letter
to be sure to make it. Anyway, I think his glacier is a
great metaphor for pastoral work, which goes for such
long stretches without anything perceptible happening.
His glacier metaphor turns the incremental nature of
pastoral and family work, the preaching and praying,
into something quite glorious. Consider the glacier
metaphor for your fortieth birthday present!

With much love,
Your Dad

THE SIXTEENTH LETTER

---

12 April 2003

Dear Eric,

We'll begin Holy Week this evening as we light
our Sabbath candles. Tomorrow we will have a proper
Palm Sunday celebration featuring Anna waving palm
branches over her birthday cake. Karen will come up
for a couple of days—she loves birthday parties. We'll
have everybody here, where we have some space to move
around.

Through the Wednesday evenings of Lent, the
Lutheran churches in the valley had a round-robin of
preachers, so we heard a different Lutheran pastor each
of the Lenten Wednesdays. Last Wednesday W____ was
back and did the final service on his home ground. And

what a welcome homecoming it was. W____, as you know, is not a really great preacher, but he is always competent—he takes the task seriously, takes the Scriptures seriously. He never talks nonsense or silliness from behind the pulpit. But these other pastors who came week after week were simply an embarrassment. They were disorganized, incoherent, tried to be cute, were innocent of any association with the Scriptures, threw in gratuitous moral advice from time to time. It was simply awful. We use the Holden Village service of song and Scripture for the liturgy, so we had good prayers and music (do you know the service? Written by Marty Haugen—we do it every Lent here), but the sermons, so-called, were, well, simply not sermons. Until W____ returned—he has never sounded so good!

I'm glad that you take preaching seriously and do it so well. That you take *worship* seriously and do that so well. Your mother and I will be praying for you as you look for someone to succeed Lynn ("succeed," not "replace"—she is irreplaceable!).[1] I anticipate that it will not be easy. Just as preaching has fallen on hard times, so has worship—most "worship leaders" that I have been exposed to in the last few years don't seem to have the faintest idea what worship is. I hope I'm not getting curmudgeonly, but it distresses me how badly the twin centering acts of the congregation—sermon and worship—are carried out in so many churches today. For so many centuries, sermon and worship provided the inviolable core of congregational identity; how does it come about that they are treated so casually, even dismissively, by so many?

I'm on the last lap of writing my basic text in spiritual theology, the section on community. So I have been rethinking everything out of the Christ Our King years. Their celebration last month of their fortieth anniversary, Mother's reading of your fortieth-birthday church letter to them,[2] having all those faces and souls assembled together those days, was very timely. And at the same time, being aware of the contemporary ecclesial atmosphere on "how to run a successful church."

Early on as pastor, I had an elitist idea of church. Much of this I inherited from my growing up Pentecostal. We didn't think any of the "regular" churches were really churches. If you didn't have the standard Pentecostal confirmations of being filled with the Spirit and enter into the self-identification of being in the vanguard of the people carrying the torch of renewal into the last days, you weren't much. It took me a long time to recognize other Christians as truly peers in following Jesus. And an even longer time—well into the years after I was ordained Presbyterian—to get rid of the inner sense of superiority and privilege.

Looking back, I think this was mixed in with admiration and appetite for radical and extreme attempts at doing Christian community really well. I don't know—had I grown up Roman Catholic—if I would have been a monk (probably a Carmelite), but I certainly would have been drawn to it. And I have always been attracted to highly disciplined communities like Church of the Saviour in Washington and Koinonia in Georgia and the Bruderhof in Germany.

When Jan and I went to Bel Air, I had vague aspirations of becoming that kind of church but with no clear plan on how to go about it. I was feeling my way, trying to keep a focus, trying to avoid conventional churchiness. And then, after two to three years, I realized that I had all these people who had no taste for anything radical or sacrificial, and nothing I did was going to change that. The parable of the wheat and tares became a major piece of pastoral reorientation for me.[3] *This* is what I had been given—wheat and tares—and I couldn't be trusted to tell one from the other, and so I had just better get on with it.

I continued to admire the radical/sacrificial/contemplative communities (and still do), but I came to accept that the normative Christian gathering into a community of the Holy Spirit was pretty much what I saw assembled before me each Sunday morning. This is what pastors are given as their field in which to work. Baptism—not keen motivation, not spiritual rigor— defines the people we preach to, pray with, listen to, and love.

Now, here's the part that I'm not so sure about. I am not sure that I have this next part right. Because of my acceptance of the "wheat and tares" congregation as normative, and because of my "cure" from Pentecostal elitism, I have been wary of renewal movements, revival rhetoric, and the enormous energy being poured into efforts to improve and perfect the church in our time. I haven't exactly been standoffish—I participate with and support Presbyterians for Renewal, for instance—but for me, at least, that is not where the action is.

This accounts, too, for my diminishing enthusiasm for parachurch movements. They leave out too much— they detour around these people who "don't get it," who are slow to jump on the bandwagon, who have contrary streaks in them. Not that they don't do much good, but without the normative congregation, which these energetic, focused, in-a-hurry people look at with considerable disdain, all you have is a lot of "special forces" companies to attack strategic strongholds. Meanwhile, who deals with the wounded, the crippled, the children, the low achievers—the majority of the people in the neighborhood?

The pastors, that's who. Treating them not as the world treats them, and not as they think of themselves, but with the dignity of souls baptized in the name of the Father, the Son, and the Holy Spirit.

The rhetoric of renewal and revival always seems to me to leave behind a lot of the people I really care about. At the same time, there is always a lurking anxiety that without it, I will reduce the gospel to the capacities or desires of the least hungry, the least motivated, the least obedient—become a chaplain to mediocrity.

Anyway, what I am trying to do in this final section on community is to deal with the church just as it is, a fact of the Holy Spirit's work, and not as we think it should be. I want to reduce as much as possible the rhetoric of "should" and replace it with the language of appreciation and wonder. And I'm finding it, to say the least, a challenge.

Be blessed, you and your congregation, this Holy Week.

With much love,
Your Dad

THE SEVENTEENTH LETTER

———

16 August 2003

Dear Eric,

In September I am going to Chicago to speak at the
Christian Century's annual dinner. I have given them
as a title "As Kingfishers Catch Fire . . . ," the opening
words of G. M. Hopkins's sonnet, with the subtitle,
"The Contemplative Christian in North America." I'm
trying to write my address before we leave for Norway
on August 26 because I won't have much time when
we return. And the picture that keeps moving to the
foreground of my imagination is that day in the middle
of July when we and several of your friends were at
Colbert Church and you were giving us a tour.

I had this deep sense of wholeness, of rightness about the church and your leadership of it as we walked around the grounds. Everything seemed to fit, to be appropriate, to somehow give expression to the gospel, to the Christian life well-lived. You have kept the center centered—worship as the defining act of the congregation, worship as the work each week of integrating the sinners into the scriptural text and celebrating with the saints the Revelation and the Presence and articulating lives of obedience and mission. In one sense, this was nothing new. Your mother and I feel this every time we worship with you, newly astonished each time at how natural and at ease it all is, so at home in this world of grace and glory. What was new in me was the realization (although I knew in my head that this had been going on) of how *missional* all this had become at Colbert. That the mission of the congregation was not added on, not an extra, but was perfectly continuous with the life of worship, and so organic with it. The vegetable garden, the prayer garden, the pavilion, the playground, the social-services outreach, your connection with the Native American congregation in Idaho. None of it contrived or self-conscious. I never managed to bring this off at COK—never developed a missional life adequate to the worship life of the congregation (although I think Linda has

made huge strides in a mature missional life in the last
few years). I don't quite know how you did it so well,
without straining, without making worship and mission
two separate things. I know it's not perfect and never
will be. All the same, it is conspicuously *there*, working
in a wonderful way. It feels very whole and accomplished
and, well, "gospel."

This doesn't happen very often in our culture, and
I am pretty sure that the reason it doesn't happen is
that it is uncommon in the church to have an adequate
and practiced *means* to accomplish our ends. For the
most part, we have an adequate theology, an adequate
organization, adequate motivation and energy. But when
it comes to means—how we will fulfill the commands,
how we will work toward the great ends (to glorify God
and enjoy him forever)—we pick up "ways and means"
from the American culture, rather than from Jesus
and Scripture. We use criteria of efficiency, statistical
results, timelines and programmatic goals, abstract
plans and principles that can be employed with a
minimum of personal, relational involvement. We use
the means that are used routinely in business, politics,
education, and sports, where they work very well. But
in the church, they result in a church that is more like
what takes place in business, politics, education, and
sports: a church, that is, without mystery, deficient

in personal relationships, in a hurry, impatient, and image-conscious. And that means that there is very little connection between worship and mission. If worship is the cultivation of who we are and what we are here for, mission has a lot to do with how we get it done. When the missional "how" is severed from the worship "who and what," the missional life no longer is controlled and shaped by Scripture and the Spirit. And so mission becomes shrill, dependent on constant "strategies" and promotional schemes. The proliferation of technology in our time exacerbates our plight—we have so many attractive options regarding the "how" that it is difficult not to use them in such a good cause as the gospel, not discerning whether or not they are appropriate to a life that is immersed in personal relationships (deriving from the Trinity) and a willingness to live in a mystery in which I am not in control. You told me once that you would be satisfied and feel you had done your job if you could just lead your parishioners to understand their baptism. I like that. The evidence is accumulating that you are doing that.

Back to the "Kingfishers . . ." lecture. This is what I want to get across as "contemplative." And that day in July as we walked around the church grounds and saw worship/mission laid out so clearly and unpretentiously and naturally (or supernaturally!) is the image that keeps informing what I am writing. A life both personally and corporately conducted in which the insides and outsides are continuous. A life in which we are as careful and attentive to the *how* as to the *what*. But we Americans (I don't know if other cultures are as negligent in this regard) keep doing the right thing in the wrong way, over and over and over again. But if we are going to live the Jesus life, we simply have to do it the Jesus way—he is, after all, the Way as well as the Truth and Life.

I want to insist that Christian congregations and their pastors need to understand themselves as the "Ways and Means Committee" of our culture. It is not so much what we do that is wrong; it is the way we do it. Until we care as much and are as careful with the means as we are the ends, what we do just makes matters worse. I anticipate using three aspects of the Christian life in which our means are frequently inappropriate: congregation, Scripture, and resurrection.

This letter is a dry run.

(An aside: I did pick up an item in your recent newsletter that I would like to discuss with you sometime. That you as pastor were one of the persons who had access to the personal giving of the members. I'm not sure that is right. I never trusted myself with that information and never knew what I might do with the information if I did have it. My concern mostly was with how it would affect my relations with those who gave a lot, rather than those who gave little. We can talk about this sometime.)

In the midst of the fires all around us (all at least fifty miles away and so not threatening us), we are enveloped in smoke. We can't see the mountains across the lake seven miles away. And with all this drama, with grand photographs and panicky headlines in the paper each morning, we had some drama of our own. We have had a pack rat for a couple of weeks. The nocturnal creature leaves our deck and our deck chairs full of pee and poop each morning. I went out and bought a live trap since he seemed to have taken up permanent residence. I got it baited and set. But we were eating late that night and sitting outside in the dark, finishing our meal, when Jan screamed her patented banshee shriek. The rat had bitten her toe—an understandably preferable morsel over the peanut butter in the trap. The apocalyptic alarm must have scared the little guy terribly because he didn't show up for three to four more nights. Two nights ago, we caught him. Last night, we caught another. When I finish this letter, I will take him down to the lake, drown him, and give him a dignified burial.

We leave for two weeks in Norway beginning on August 26.

I still haven't finished *Christ Plays*—only thirty or so pages left, but I can't seem to get them written.

Summer isn't turning out to be a congenial season for writing! What we need is some several weeks of drizzle. That would do it, I think: Stop the fires and start my imagination.

With much love, Eric,

Dad

THE EIGHTEENTH LETTER

—

22 October 2003

Dear Eric,

It is a long time since I've written—too long. I have
not been vigilant enough in saying no to well-meaning
people and invitations. And to complicate things, I have
now developed a hernia (did I tell you that?). It popped
out just as we were getting ready to leave for Norway.
So I just kept holding it in, hoping it wouldn't strangle.
But I have a date for surgery now—next Wednesday, the
twenty-ninth. There is some cosmic unfairness in all
this. Here I am, keeping my body active all these years,
and virtually everything that can go wrong has gone
wrong: tonsils, appendicitis, knee cartilage, prostate,
two cataracts, nose, hernia on the left side, and now

another hernia on the right. And your mother, who, as a nice Southern girl, always sang in the glee club instead of playing games (so she wouldn't perspire!), has only gone to the hospital to have three babies.

I don't quite know how we managed to get caught in so much travel, coming and going, these last two and a half months. After Norway/Sweden, we had hardly gotten our feet on the ground when I went to Chicago and the Christian Century lectures. Then I picked up Jan and we went to Maine to the seaside cottage of some friends for a holiday, and then spent some time with the pastors in the area (our host was a Baptist pastor), then went to Philipsburg, Pennsylvania, to preach the installation of Tracie, then on to western Pennsylvania for a Wee Kirk pastors' conference. Jan and I left this one feeling depressed—they all seemed so trivial and, well, unserious. I wondered what in the world I was doing there. Tough as pastoral work is, there is still an inherent dignity in it in even the hardest of places—but you would never know it in that crowd. We came back feeling more isolated than ever. We'd hardly gotten home when four pastors came for a couple of days to "talk." They left yesterday noon and a man from Calgary called and wanted to take us to supper last night—so he motorcycled down and talked for three hours nonstop. We are not managing this life in the contemplative Promised Land of Canaan very well.

Our Norway trip felt like a pilgrimage, getting the feel for that country, its fjords and mountains, and getting the music of its language into our imaginations. It revived my interest in the novels of Sigrid Undset—we spent a couple of days in her old neighborhood. She wrote two huge historical novels on medieval Norway, *Kristin Lavransdatter* (three volumes) and *The Master of Hestviken* (four volumes), which I read thirty years ago.

Have you read her? She was raised in a rationalist home; her novels, as she was writing them, brought her to conversion (Roman Catholic). The revisiting of her life and surroundings was timely. I loved her novels when I first read them, so full of deep reflections on sin and redemption, so nuanced with observations on sanctity, on holy lives. She received the Nobel Prize somewhere around 1928 and became famous. She quit her novel writing and started writing about saints, and then went out propagandizing for the Catholic faith and hating the Nazis, who invaded her country and killed her son. She came to America and deteriorated into an opinionated, bitter, mean-spirited woman who traded in that marvelous imagination and Christ-saturated passion for plodding, didactic saint stories and anti-Nazi speechmaking.

It is this old pastoral puzzle writ large: How does someone who knows so much and has such a complete and seemingly thoroughly assimilated gospel faith through much suffering (divorced, Undset raised five children—two of them mentally ill or impaired—by herself, much of the time in poverty) end up like that? But it does happen.

At times this faith life, this Christ Kingdom life, seems so strong and impregnable—such a solid bulwark against vanity and triviality. And at other times, like when considering Undset, it seems so fragile, so vulnerable to being seductively undermined by subtle, unnoticed temptations, bringing some of the best people we know to shipwreck. I think some of the same thing happened to Luther—so robust and imaginative, so energetic and sharply focused. And then as an old man obese and arrogant, surrounded by adoring sycophants. Kierkegaard remarked that in those last years, every time he farted, he thought it was the Holy Ghost speaking.

In making these observations, which I've been thinking about a lot lately, I realized how dangerous this pastoral work is in which you and I are engaged—and how we are never out of danger. Or maybe just when we think we are out of danger, we are in the most danger.

Jan requested a poem for our forty-fifth wedding anniversary in August. Did I show it to you? I've made some revisions to it; I think it is finished. And since you are substantially involved in it, I wanted you to have it.

The peace of our Lord and with much love,

Dad

THE MAKING OF
SELAH HOUSE

———

For our forty-fifth wedding anniversary,
2 August 2003

1

Once upon a time
—it was the first time we saw each other—
We saw and heard the other singing. Eyes
And voices met on just the right
Notes. A marriage tune
Composed itself and we've
Been singing it ever since. Not
Always on key, but the melody
Has carried us well enough.
It wasn't so very long ago.

2

Once upon a time
We lived at 300 Pennsylvania
Avenue, moved to 43 Barker and became
Parents and pastors. We shared 1321
Saratoga Drive with a congregation of sinners.
Highland Avenue gave us refuge,
2233 Allison Road a nesting until 397
Hughes Bay Road welcomed us
To Selah House for dwelling and abiding.
It was a long time ago.

3

Once upon a time
The Spirit breathed on forty-six lumps
Of clay in our suburban catacomb
And a No-people became a People. Mildred
Little and Ken Seiple were not our pick for Jachin
And Boaz, flanking our resurrection Temple,
But there they were, God's choice.
We swallowed our disappointment
And got on with it: "Let us worship God."
It wasn't so very long ago.

4

Once upon a time
We climbed above the tree line
And observed our marriage
From a pile of Canadian rocks
—a marriage on the rocks—perched
Above an alpine lake, named for
Bertha, a frontier mountain whore.
Hospitable solitude for realizing
The one flesh we were becoming.
It was a long time ago.

5

Once upon a time
We took a Monday Sabbath walk
Along the Little Gunpowder, silent
In the company of singing vireos
And kingfishers, prayerful in the

Company of the Holy Trinity.
Over decades the sabbath trail branched out
To Sooke Harbour, Katahdin, and Siyeh
Pass, still keeping silence, still praying.
It wasn't so very long ago.

6

Once upon a time
The doctors poked and probed
Our bodies looking for death.
They took our blood and cut
Our flesh, x-rayed our gut and gave
Us pills, hooked us up to machines
And suggested that if we drank six
Glasses of water a day
We just might live forever.
It was a long time ago.

7

Once upon a time
Our parents and two sisters died,
Three in the east and three in the west.
We grieved and were grateful and gave
Witness to the resurrection. They
Gave us a "goodly heritage."
We marvel the ways those deaths
Continue to sow life in us. We're
Living off of a rich inheritance.
It wasn't so very long ago.

8

Once upon a time
We brewed morning mugs of
Prayer coffee from fresh ground
Beans, kept a eucharistic kitchen,
Ventured into Pad Thai, filling
The house with exotic Asian
Aromatics, and weekdays prepared
Bowls of oatmeal to maintain
A firm foundation in the ordinary.
It was a long time ago.

9

Once upon a time
A child was conceived in our bed,
And then another and another and another.
Named in love and baptized
In the Name of Father Son and Holy Spirit.
These miracle others, a faculty of the Trinity,
Trained us in the trinitarian way
To live by receiving and love,
By accepting all in Jesus' name.
It wasn't so very long ago.

10

Once upon a time
A glacier one mile thick carved
The rock on which our Selah House
Is built. Floods came and left

This light-filled meditation pool
That waters our prayers and keeps
Us, body and soul, baptismal clean.
Sometimes we see tongues of fire.
Sometimes we hear angels' wings.
It was a long time ago.

THE NINETEENTH LETTER

—

11 January

Baptism of Our Lord 2004

Dear Eric,

W____ also preached on baptism this morning. But my mind was filled with what you were doing and saying, and I might not have given him my full attention. The more I hear you talk about baptism, the more I think you have found a focus that is essential for your congregation—for all of our congregations—these days: to realize the totally *personal* nature of our lives as given in our naming, and to realize the totally *relational* nature of our lives given in the naming of the Trinity, the divine community in which we find our being, our identity.

And who else is there in the neighborhood to say that, to remind people of this, and to continue to *do* it—to

baptize these people in the Name and then continue
to treat them consistently as nothing other or less than
baptized? Nobody. Nobody but us, the pastors. Not that
nobody else can do it, but nobody is in the strategic
position of continual reflection on nurturing these
countercultural identities. We do the baptizing, but
we also are the ones who are entrusted to treat them
as baptized, as these personal/relational beings who
are created and re-created in the image of the three-
personed God. Isn't the most conspicuous need in our
culture today to find ways of recovering personal and
relational identity, to develop strategies of countering the
insistent and insidious depersonalizing, derelationalizing
forces of darkness that pervade our schools, our
government, our entertainment, our finances? And
doesn't the church betray the very grounds of its
existence when it adopts ways of worship and program
and mission that are impersonal and individualistic?

You have thought this through far more thoroughly
than I did at your age, and I now wonder how I could
have missed something so obvious. But at least I can ride
on your coattails as you do some remedial baptismal
work in the church that I didn't quite get. And for that,
I'm thankful. Thank *you*!

After worship today, we drove up to Big Mountain
to see what we could see. I haven't been up there in the

winter since I was eighteen. Three or four times in the summer, but not with the place deep in snow and piled high with skiers. This is where I learned to ski—there were no outbuildings, just a warming lodge with coffee and hot chocolate, a rope lift for children and a T-bar for adults and two slopes—the bunny hill and the main slope. Now there are condominiums and elaborate homes all over the place, chairlifts and gondolas, and skiing slopes past imagining. Signs of conspicuous wealth everywhere. And, of course, filled parking lots. We found a little lunch place, had a bowl of soup, and left. It was like being in a crowded shopping mall.

Driving home, I was struck by the huge change in atmosphere and culture in this place that was significant for me fifty years ago from what it is now. And I wonder if I quite comprehend the significance of the change. And if I have enough of a feel for what men and women are experiencing in these so different conditions to qualify me to write books to guide them in living a holy life. Oddly, I have never felt so incompetent to write on what is involved in following Jesus in the context of this culture, and yet, even more oddly, I feel a drive, an energy, to keep writing. I still feel most like a pastor when I write, and I guess that is why I do it. But I hope the pastor who is writing is not stuck in the conditions on Big Mountain of fifty years ago.

Here is another pastoral observation. Your mother
has been spending a lot of time lately with a woman
in our congregation who has cancer, has thrice weekly
sessions with a physical therapist for a replaced hip,
and has regular chemo sessions. Jan is not the only one
helping out, but she is probably the one who has the most
personal and prayerful relationship with her. I know that
I cannot help this woman, but I experience something
like a deep delight as Jan does it. I'm still getting to be
a pastor vicariously. It just surprises me how much I feel
this, how much it means to me to still be a hands-on
pastor, through Jan. I suspect that that is what I feel in
regard to you, also. I know I cannot do it any longer
except in bits and pieces. Nor do I want to. But I must
miss it more than I have been conscious of since I take
such delight in what you are doing and in what Jan has
been doing these last couple of weeks.

The peace of our Lord,

Dad

THE TWENTIETH LETTER

——

6 February 2004

Dear Eric,

Welcome home from Hawaii! Now you have our appetites whetted.

This is just a quick note on some things you have written:

> The newsletter report on your baptism sermon. You did the story justice, and then some! A card-carrying member of the company of storytellers! Your Eutychus reports. That is a great format to work out of—a creative way to get information and images into the minds/hearts of your congregation. Keep them going . . .

And the letter to the congregation regarding Lynn's
stepping down from the worship leadership. You
expressed that so well and conveyed so much of
the nature of your marriage and your co-ministry.
I really liked it—both personal and pastoral.

Your mother and I read these things, usually aloud,
and fill with pride—but not the sin kind!

Love,

Dad

THE TWENTY-FIRST LETTER

———

31 May 2004

Dear Eric,

Pentecost yesterday, today Memorial Day. A nice
juxtaposition of the ecclesial and the secular. Yesterday
we worshipped; today we are just taking time to do some
chores, fool around, read—an aimless, meandering day
that we probably don't do often enough. We started
out by bringing the fuchsia and other flower baskets
down from the garage to hang them, but I have now
put them all back—it is cold and a strong wind is coming
in off the lake, so we better not risk it. So now I am
stretched out in the living room with my laptop on
my lap and writing to you. I have gone through all the
Eric-Timothy Letters to get a feel for what has been

accumulating. The first was written on Christmas Day 1999. And this is number twenty-one—three-and-a-half years of reflections on being a pastor in relation to you as a pastor. A good thing for me to do. Thanks for suggesting it.

One of the impressions that I have overall is what a privileged work this is. I know that every work has its own glory and uniqueness. But this vocation is such an immersion in the local, the personal, the relational, the scriptural, the spiritual—so rich in detail and beauty, so alive with variety and interest, and also so dangerous, requiring vigilance and wariness. But I realize also that many of our colleagues don't have this experience at all—that they experience pastoral work as a series of dead ends. I don't quite know how to account for that.

We just had a couple of overnight guests, longtime friends whom we haven't seen for twenty years, on their way to Seattle to a new job. One of the decisions they are faced with is a new church. I suggested Bethany on Queen Anne Hill, and they responded, "Oh no—it has to be a large church; we need a large church." I didn't say anything, but what I felt was that they were prideciding against and ruling out what is most characteristic and unique about the church—the local, the personal, the relational. And choosing instead the impersonal, homogenized blandness, performance, the gospel-in-general, one-size-fits-all sermons and programs, a congregation in which they could pick whatever friends they wanted and avoid easily everyone else and probably never have a pastor who knew them and whom they knew.

Your mother and I are reading (out loud in the evenings) a new novel sent to us by a friend: Jeff Berryman's *Leaving Ruin*.[1] A first novel about an evangelical Texas pastor in the town of Ruin. The writer is not himself a pastor, but he certainly knows pastor and congregation life in detail—and it is so well-written. It is not a happy story in one sense—he is being kicked out of his church after nine years—but in reading it, I realize why I feel so lucky to have been a pastor: There is so much meaning inherent in virtually every detail of this life, and there is so much at stake in every life, including the pastor's. Plenty of ugliness and meanness, but also amazing grace and unsuspected beauty. I have always found pastor/church novels to be ways of noticing and appreciating the complexities involved in this work and a confirmation of the essential dignity involved in our calling. Important because we are often the victims of stereotypes and condescension, since we are not easily seen as contributing to the economy. This novel is right up there with Georges Bernanos's *The Diary of a Country Priest*, Graham Greene's *The Power and the Glory*, Edwin

O'Connor's *The Edge of Sadness*, Harold Frederic's *The Damnation of Theron Ware*, Dostoevsky's *The Brothers Karamazov*. And many more. It always astonishes me that writers who have never lived this life can know, through their imaginations, so much about it—and get it so accurately. Understand the manifold subtleties of sin and holiness in congregations and their pastors. As I think about this now, in retrospect, I think that the novel has been a major source of insight for me into the unique qualities that come together in our pastoral vocations.

One of the losses that Jan and I have felt now that Miles and Karen have retired from the Polson church is the termination of the wonderful baptism stories that kept coming out of that place. Lutherans and Presbyterians who mostly baptize infants just can't match them. But a few Sundays ago at Eidsvold, we had one that at least deserves honorable mention. Four families were presenting their children for baptism. I didn't know any of them, and it looked like all the parents were all brothers and sisters. One mother was without a husband. All the children were about two years old and being held by a parent. But the child of the single mother was squirmy, and she finally gave up and set him down. He wandered off, exploring behind the pulpit, climbed on the communion rail—this was obviously totally new territory for him, and he was checking out all the details.

When time came for the act of baptism, he was down
with the congregation, and his mother motioned to him
to come up. He was disoriented, out of place, didn't
know what was going on, and as he went up the chancel
steps nervously tugged at his trousers and pulled them
down. At the top step, he bent over and mooned the
congregation!

Maybe the baptismal-story well is not yet dried up.

With much love,

Dad

THE TWENTY-SECOND LETTER

---

24 January 2005

Dear Eric,

Since we got home last week the freezing rain has continued daily, wreaking havoc on the roads, melting the snow, and breaking up the ice on the bay. All that stunning winter beauty that we were relishing has vanished into puddles of mud. Two weeks ago, I was regretting that we had scheduled our Hawaii holiday at this time of year when there is so much winter to exult in. But with what we are in for now, Hawaii looks pretty good. We leave on Monday.

Being with you and your kids was very good for us. And being in your pulpit was a good thing for me. You had mentioned earlier how you were surprised how few times I had preached for your congregation. But I think it has been just right—your mother and I have felt really privileged to be there at significant occasions, but I have always felt I was just there as one of the family and not a special feature. So thank you for that. You were right in your surmise that I wasn't treated as a celebrity—I was just your dad, and that seemed totally appropriate.

The timing was important too. I am in the middle, as you know, of this third spirituality book, *Follow the Leader*, a conversation on spiritual leadership.[1] Worshipping with your congregation was breathing fresh air. Everything seems so *healthy* in your sanctuary: the spirit, the aesthetics, the music, the architecture, the people . . . everything. And I came away realizing how rare this is in America these days, how demoralized (judging from my mailbag) pastors are, and how congregations have gotten so trivialized by panicky attempts to be "effective" and "relevant."

Anyway, back to the book: What I experienced in your sanctuary was an immersion in a healthy, mature congregation and healthy, mature worship. And it brought me back to my writing desk here with a deepened conviction of both how rare this is but also how available it is if we just pay attention to what we have already been given.

The basic structure of the book contrasts the leadership of Jesus with Herod, Caiaphas, and Josephus, and then further with the Pharisees, the Essenes, and the Zealots. That part is basically lectures I have given at Regent. But as I got started again on this, I felt that I needed to work out the way of Jesus—the leadership way of Jesus—much more substantially before dealing with the contrasts. So I picked out six "ways," ways of leadership that are basically either ignored or rejected in politics, business, and church in America, but that together more or less make up the way of Jesus: Abraham climbing Moriah, Moses on the plains of Moab, David in the cave at En-gedi, Elijah beside the brook Cherith, Isaiah of Jerusalem in the field of stumps, and Isaiah of the Exile by the waters of Babylon. Together these will amount to the first half of the book—150 or so pages.

Abraham proved harder than I anticipated—I had you send me Kierkegaard to give me some guidance. S. K.[2] meant a lot to me years ago, and I thought when I first read *Fear and Trembling* that it was the last word on Abraham and Isaac. But after you sent it (I intended to just skim it, but that proved impossible), I began to have second thoughts about it. What had stuck with me from S. K. was this deep, extended immersion in the Abraham/ Moriah story that recovered the radical implications of

LETTERS TO A YOUNG PASTOR

faith in an ecclesiastical world that is very much like ours.
So far, so good.

But what strikes me now is that S. K. wrote this (or
at least published it) when he was thirty years old. Two
years earlier, he had broken his engagement with his
fiancée, Regine, and he seems to me now to have been
obsessively writing himself into the Moriah story, making
Regine stand for Isaac and putting himself in the person
of Abraham. Here's what impresses me now: However
important Kierkegaard is for reclaiming the essential
radicalness of the gospel—and I think he is—he was not
a very healthy person emotionally, and especially in the
affair of Regine, he seems to me to be downright neurotic.
Fear and Trembling strikes me this time around as biblical
interpretation catalyzed by neurosis. After spending six
weeks or so writing eighteen pages on Abraham at Moriah
now, I've come to the conclusion that I don't trust S. K.—
on this one anyway. Too much Regine got into the mix.

And this is where you come in, you and your
congregation. After all those weeks trying to find my
way through S. K.'s brilliant but neurotic (as it seems to
me) approach to the way of faith, the health of Colbert
(and its pastor!) just hit me with a welcoming sense of
gladness and wholeness.

I don't think I can do without people like S. K.—he
makes it impossible to trivialize this life, this gospel

life. And for that, I'll always be in his debt. But he does something else that I am now suspicious of: He overdramatizes faith, *melo*dramatizes it and himself along with it. I can't live at that pitch; neither can the people to whom I'm pastor and for whom I write. There has to be a healthier, a *holier* alternative to the appalling silliness that has permeated American religion than S. K.

Do you know why I trust your witness and comments on these matters and don't trust S. K.? Because you are a pastor and are spending your life in the trenches with people who suffer, providing patient and prayerful counsel, hanging on all the time to the presence of Jesus, trying to stay honest to the Scriptures, showing up in worship with people who arrive dragging doubts with occasional lunges toward trust. While S. K., in contrast, cut himself off from everybody and endlessly dramatized himself theologically. The fact is that every sentence in the Genesis text on Abraham (chapter 22) understates whatever is going on—no hysterics, no drama, nothing extreme. Quite matter-of-fact. We, in our attempt to enter into the story and psychologize it, imagine the terror and the abyss—the S. K. "absurd"—but the text doesn't do that. Anyway, I've ended up using S. K. more as a foil than a mentor in this faith business.

The rest of the week we'll spend getting ready for Hawaii—no great preparations, mostly getting the right stuff to wear and read—and (for me) abandoning the routines (and computer!) that make life so congenial here. Maybe we'll see a ram in the thicket along the way. And maybe we won't.

The peace of our Lord and much, much love,

Dad

THE TWENTY-THIRD LETTER

—

14 May 2005

Eve of Pentecost

Dear Eric,

Tomorrow is Pentecost. And I'm thinking about you right now, praying you into your pulpit. Most Sundays I don't think about missing it—the sermon and sacrament and all that. But Pentecost is one of the exceptions—a kind of nostalgic ache: "Oh, I wish I was in the middle of that again." I don't know what it is about Pentecost Sunday. Maybe because I grew up Pentecostal and then later in life felt that they had gotten it all wrong—the nature of the event, the deep continuities with every ordinary gathering of God's people—and how glad I was to get to celebrate and preach those continuities with my congregation. Sometimes I fantasize about getting up

early some Pentecost Sunday and driving to Spokane to
sit in your study, robed and ready to preach. You walk
in on me, totally surprised. I tell you, "Sorry, Eric, I'm
preaching today—take your place in the congregation."
And you do it.

We are leaving Wednesday for a week: We go to
Seattle for an evening meeting for a Regent event. On to
Vancouver for another. (These are in relation to a major
Regent fundraising campaign of several million dollars
to build a new library for the school. Your mom and I
are "honorary chairpersons," if you can believe that.)
And then two lectures on Saturday: "Practice Death"
(Abraham on Moriah—exploring the details of the way
of faith as defined by sacrifice); "Practice Resurrection"
(naming the ordinary circumstances in which resurrection occurs in the months between Easter sunrise
services). I had originally imagined this as eighty days of
purpose: forty days of death/Lent with Abraham, and
forty days of resurrection/Easter with Jesus. Thought
maybe I could trump the Saddleback people. But my
public-relations/financial advisors tell me it's too late.

We will be just in and out of Regent. As much as we
have appreciated the Regent place and community, it's
not good for my soul to hang around that kind of place.
We are going to stay with Craig and Julie Gay overnight
and then hightail it to Sooke Harbour on Vancouver

Island for two nights and then take the Anacortes
ferry on the way home. We'll meet Karen and Dave on
Wednesday for a birthday dinner at Perugia (Karen's
birthday is Thursday), and then get home on Thursday.

I've been rereading Martin Buber the last few weeks.
I've learned so much from him through the years, and
every once in a while, I need a refresher course. In some
ways it seems strange—here is a Jew who comes off the
page as a brother in Christ, a friend that I keep having
resonating conversations with. The refreshing thing, I
think, is that he writes like an evangelical Christian but
without the evangelical clichés, the jargon. So I get a
conversation partner, not unlike you, who is nourishing
without having to spit out the bones every turn of the
page. The book I am working my way through is an old
one, a collection of essays, *Israel and the World*.[1]

And here's another: Annie Proulx, *The Shipping News*.[2]
It was left behind by a guest. It won the Pulitzer or
National Book Award ten years or so ago.[3] Leif told me
he didn't like it. But we started it one evening just to get
a feel for it. It was awful—the corruption and sordidness—
but we agreed to give it fifty pages. I'm glad we did:
Above the moral chaos and spiritual abyss, the dove
began to hover, and page after page, it is as if the voice
starts each day with "Let there be . . ." We're nearly
done now and have this whole cast of characters who

are finding their way by means of a kind of gutsy grace. Isn't it a huge irony that we find our distinctive pastor identity most often confirmed and elaborated by writers who don't have born-again press cards stuck in their hat bands?

And yet another. Did I tell you about Marilynne Robinson's *Gilead*?[4] This one is openly, identifiably Christian: a long, book-length letter of an aging, dying pastor to his seven-year-old son. He has been a pastor all his life in a small church in the small Iowan town of Gilead. He knows that he will be dead soon and wants his son to know who he is/was. And so he tells him in this letter that the son will have to read when he grows up. The life of a pastor—this out-of-the-way life that is so rich in beauty and pain and redemption, totally unpretentious, and absolutely honest. Not a single false note that I detected. It is some kind of miracle that it has been acclaimed by the secular press. Maybe those pagan publishers and reviewers in New York are not so much hostile or indifferent to the Christian faith as they are to shoddiness and cheapness.

And not so incidentally, while we are on books: Leif's novel, *Catherine Wheels*, is scheduled for publication, as you know, in September from Waterbrook Press.[5] He has been seven years writing this book (the only work, I'm sure, that rivals pastor work in its immersion

in painstaking, slowly accumulating detail is that of
the novelist). The publisher asked me to write an
endorsement for it. Which I am glad to do—I'm hoping
that nobody except his friends will connect us as son
and father. Maybe I should suggest to the publisher that
they ask you also for an endorsement—round up all the
pastoral support that our family can muster! Here's what
I have written:

> I read good novelists to keep our great
> words—*holy, salvation, hope, trust, miracle, saint*—
> specific and *lived.* Not abstract. Not churchy.
> Leif Peterson's *Catherine Wheels* does this
> convincingly: One after another, men and
> women who have quit on life are led back to
> life by a nine-year-old, saint-christened girl,
> each one a believable Christ-resurrection that
> could be, and probably is, taking place in
> your neighborhood right now.

It is easy to get bitchy about the state of pastoring and
worship and church these days. I try to keep my tongue
on a tight leash. But sometimes, someone shows up here
that relieves me from being cautious—someone who
comes in here with maturity, redolent with ozone, and
I feel glad to be numbered in the company of pastors,

without apology, without reservation. Oscar spent a
couple of days with us last week. I have known him
for twenty years. He has always pastored small Baptist
churches here in Montana but now is in Ohio. A talented
preacher and pastor, but also deliberate about not
"climbing the ladder." Being a pastor has never been easy
for him; he is a manic-depressive and is frequently and
seriously suicidal (although he has mastered a persona
that masks his interior stuff quite well); three children
that he got through college on his meager salaries; two
years ago, a grandchild from an unmarried daughter,
given up for adoption. His wife, lovely, but harassed by
autoimmune disease. You get the picture: natural gifts,
but practiced in difficult circumstances, both exterior
and interior. But what a pleasure to have these couple of
days with him last week. He is one of the truly *healthy*
pastors I have the pleasure of knowing. A pastor who
gives dignity to his congregations—treats each person
with the affection of a novelist, relishing the details,
praying the uniqueness. He is fascinated right now with
Bonhoeffer on preaching. Bonhoeffer (I never heard
this) often told his students that when they preached,
even if it wasn't a very good sermon, Jesus was walking
up and down the aisles healing and comforting and
saving people. And he meant it quite literally. After he
left, I realized something I had never named before: that

in a line of work in which so many pastors we meet have this deep sense of insecurity, compensated for in so many unlovely ways, Oscar is totally comfortable with himself *just as he is.*

The days after he left, the phrase kept running through my head, "There are yet seven thousand who have not bowed the knee to Baal . . ."[6] And we are lucky enough to get to know some of them. Isn't that great?

Your mother and I are thinking, imagining, praying you into your sabbatical. It is so necessary for you at this time.

The peace of our Lord,

Dad

THE TWENTY-FOURTH
LETTER

—

15 October 2005

Twenty-First Week after Pentecost

Dear Eric,

Your mother and I are still enjoying the aftershocks of ecstasy from the award of the sabbatical grant. We are both feeling keenly the accumulated fatigue that you continue to feel. And we pray. I am not sure I have ever felt such a continuous stream of intercession working within me, as in this transitional time in your pastor/ family/whatever/life.

In remembering back through the Christ Our King years, my midforties carried a sense of vulnerability with them. There was a feeling of—I don't quite know what to name it—maybe being imperiled. By this time, the congregation was fairly well established. I had a couple of books (*Long Obedience* and *Five Smooth Stones*) published, and the adrenaline was down. I had lived for twelve years or so with a challenge, with a defined task, and with a strong motivation not to fail. I was also learning how to be a pastor and had gone from knowing virtually nothing to at least knowing the contours and dimensions involved in being a pastor. Also, I was becoming accustomed to parenthood—the miracle of being a father was no longer a constant surprise. I wouldn't say I was exactly bored, but there was a leveling off; life was not as high-energy. The word that occurs to me right now was a kind of *slackness*. The temptation—and I think I identified it as such at the time—was to create new challenges, venture into new territories, which at the same time I knew were not part of my vocation, had nothing to do with the life I had been given but could only weaken or interfere with it.

I was not as insightful as you are being in doing something about it. I think I just kind of muddled through. I got Sister Constance as my spiritual director—that provided a kind of regular clarification that had marks of the Spirit in it. With the encouragement of an elder (Thad Kelly—do you remember him, a medical doctor at Hopkins?), I worked out with the session two months away every summer, a month of vacation plus a month of writing leave: two months in Montana!

That was significant. And I quit working so hard. I was with a group of Presbyterian pastors last month at Glacier Camp's Spruce Lodge for a few days, and one of them asked what I would have done differently when I was their age (these were all first-call pastors). My spontaneous answer was, "I would work only half as much." If I had thought beforehand, I might not have said that, but I think it is true. Too much of what I did was because I didn't know what to do and didn't want to appear incompetent, just standing around doing nothing.

It seems to me that you are being much more deliberate and wise in dealing with the fatigue you have found enervating you: your new spiritual director, the Thursday sermon time in the protected cave of the Whitworth Library, the reduction of preaching to three Sundays a month, building the kayak with Lindsay last winter, a readiness to "escape" when the occasion offers, as in your fishing trip recently, and, of course, the careful preparations you made in applying for the Lilly grant.

One of the standard solutions to stagnation-fatigue and the accompanying banalities of mid-careerism for pastors is to change congregations. I'm glad that you are not considering that (although I'm sure that it has crossed your mind!). Almost always (but not always) that is a cheap solution and prevents a deepening of your life in the Spirit, both personally and vocationally. Did you know that the monks in contemplative orders (Benedictine and Carmelite) have a word for this? "The destruction that wastes at noonday" was what they called it.[1] I came across that when I was in the middle of it, and it helped to know that this happens often enough to those of us who are in "holy orders" to have a name. It is not necessarily a sign that I am doing something wrong, which would mean that there must be a "solution" to it.

I finished my book last week with the chapter on Josephus. I've changed the title from *Follow the Leader: A Conversation on Spiritual Leadership* to *The Way of Jesus: A Conversation on the Ways That Jesus Is the Way*.[2] Jon Stine (my old editor on *The Message*) is reading this and objected furiously to the first title. I was reluctant to give it up, as I have had it in my head for ten years or so now. How would you like it if your wife or pastor or best friend came to you and said, "*Sadie Lynn* is not the right name for your third child. You have to change it; find something more appropriate." That's the way I felt—but he finally persuaded me.

I have two and a half months left to go over it and incorporate Jon's edits and get it as right as I can get it. This week I have been working on an insertion on Jesus. It suddenly struck me that the key passage in calling attention to the ways that Jesus is the Way is the wilderness-temptation story. Each temptation has to do with the *way* that Jesus is going to be the Way: Is he going to reduce and depersonalize the way into providing for needs (bread)? Is he going to reduce and depersonalize the way into providing for entertainment (jumping off the Temple into the arms of angels— miracles to add excitement to life)? Is he going to reduce and depersonalize the way into a bureaucracy that will ensure peace and justice for the world (using his power to get rid of sin and evil)?

The theme that I want to pick up is that everything that the devil offered was a good thing: food, excitement, a decent government. But everything also was impersonal, enacted without love or intimacy or participation. Which are the hallmarks of the devil's ways. We cannot follow the way of Jesus but then do it any old way we like; we cannot do the Lord's work in the devil's ways. Doing good work in impersonal ways also seems to be a characteristic of American ways.

Here's the big news: We have a Jan-Birthday-Trip planned for the end of this month. We are flying to Seattle for three nights, staying in the Edgewater Hotel (which a friend tells me is the finest hotel in Seattle, downtown on the water). The same friend has also provided us with all the information for music and theater events. We have talked about doing this for years but never just up and did it. I think Jan is looking forward to it.

Patty Rath and Louise Wheatley from Maryland were with us last week for four nights, with some nice hikes and enriching conversation. We enjoyed them, but it is also nice to have our space back. We have replaced our conversations with them by reading aloud the hour before supper Wallace Stegner's *The Big Rock Candy Mountain*—we both read it thirty-five years ago—and are finding it an amazing character development in the "Western" culture that still influences a lot of what is going on around us.[3]

Much love, Eric, as you work and love . . .

Dad

THE TWENTY-FIFTH LETTER

---

3 January 2006
Tenth Day of Christmas

Dear Eric,

My first letter of the new year.

Received your church newsletter, in which you interpreted your upcoming sabbatical to the congregation, a few days ago. Your mother and I marvel at the ways you do these things. You have developed a style of conversation with the congregation that is so—well—personal, intimate, trusting. You give them so much dignity, treat them with honor. I think the reason I notice it—virtually every month—is that this pastoral tone is so rare in what I read and hear from pastors: Their language is either informational or motivational, but rarely personal. Pastor as instructor, or pastor as cheerleader, or pastor as organizer, or pastor as vision caster. But rarely pastor as companion in pilgrimage, partner in this complex and demanding business of being a congregation.

I preached an ordination sermon a couple of weeks ago in Oklahoma City for Bill Wiseman (the son of the Bill Wiseman that we worked with in White Plains). I used the John texts on Thomas. The first when he asked, "We don't know where you are going; how can we know the way?" And the second at the Resurrection appearance, when he exclaimed, "My Lord and my God!"[1] The ordination was on the Feast of St. Thomas. So I used Thomas to explore the relation of priest and people—a symbiotic relationship—both giving to and receiving from the other, the mutual giving and receiving basically consisting of asking questions because we don't know or understand what Jesus is doing/saying, and worshipping ("My Lord and my God!") when Jesus unexpectedly appears and our questions disappear in an act of surprised worship. And if we stick at this long enough, the worship finally trumps the questions. But what I wanted to emphasize is that the people/priest relationship operated between those poles, back and forth. It gave me a good dynamic to work with, and I think it worked. But I am telling you about it now because you were in the back of my mind as the working model of this: deliberately assuming a stance and attitude with the congregation on "level ground," the back-and-forthness of companionable and relaxed respect.

I've told you before how difficult it is for me to preach any more without a congregation, and so I don't do it. But this felt the way preaching is supposed to feel: totally in context, with rich personal associations holding the sentences in a kind of intimacy and gospel texture.

Bill is an interesting person. When we left White Plains, he was in high school. I think I told you about the chance/providential meeting with him in Port Aransas, Texas, a couple of years ago. Since then he has kept in touch. He is sixty-one years old and finally is becoming a pastor, which he now feels that he has been dodging and avoiding all his life. He spent a lot of time in politics—the Oklahoma legislature and a failed run for governor. And three failed marriages. But a lot of mover-and-shaker kind of stuff. And now finds that he wants to take the lowest rung and the least influential role in society and spend whatever years he has left in serving the powerless and disaffected.

I was glad to be asked to be part of this—his father played an important place in my life in the three years before we went to Bel Air. Preaching at the ordination felt like it was a part of a much larger story.

I sent off the manuscript for *The Way of Jesus* on Thursday (publication sometime in the fall). On Friday, *Eat This Book* arrived (a copy is in the mail for you).[2] I am so glad to get to write the books—they feel so much like a gathering up of what I have been doing all my life. I work hard on them, of course, but it is quite wonderful the way the material just seems to be sitting there, waiting to be shaped into a conversation with my generation.

Leif and Amy got back from their Ohio Christmas trip on Friday, dropped their kids off here on Saturday, and went for their annual New Year's Eve gathering with their friends at a lake near Eureka, returned on Sunday afternoon here for supper, and stayed over through lunch on Monday. Hans and Anna and Mary were full of life, as usual, and provided plenty of energy to get the new year launched in noisy style. Who needs fireworks?

But all that grandchildren energy didn't launch me into the new year in grand style. I feel slack and muddled. I keep thinking about the next book, *Tell It Slant*,[3] but think I will let it go for a week or two. Straighten up my files, clean my drawers, chop some wood, write letters, sharpen the kitchen knives. We saw the DVD *Winged Migration* a few days ago and really liked it. I got the video of *My Big Fat Greek Wedding* last night and will view it this afternoon. And we plan to go see *Narnia* this week in Kalispell. Fool around long enough, and the energy is bound to start bubbling up!

I've been thinking a lot in the last several months about the American church—provoked by *The Way of*

Jesus. And the huge chasm between my own experience
in the church and the cultural manifestations of it in the
Bush-dominated rhetoric and the Big Church bravado
and flashiness. My experience is basically with three
congregations: Christ Our King, Eidsvold, and Colbert. I
assume there are a lot more of them like this all over the
country and world. But these are the ones I know—and
what I know is that there is good, faithful, solid, Jesus-
honoring work going on in ways that glorify God and
contribute substantially to the growth of the Kingdom
in the world. I am glad that I got to be part of this aspect
of gospel work and living. But when I look around me
and see the societal image of the church, it seems to me
to be actually demonic—a parody of the gospel, and a
venue for vanity, and an enormous amount of silliness. An
anti-Christ church. My experience of the church seems so
totally at odds with this public expression of the church.
The interesting thing right now when I think about this
is that it doesn't bother me all that much. Somehow, my
feeling is that the public church is mostly illusion, sleight-
of-hand work at the behest of the devil and his angels, a
huge distraction to the unconnected, bored, consumerist
population. Is it naive of me to be convinced that there
are enough of these unpretentious congregations in most
of the neighborhoods of the country to act as leaven and

keep the gospel available and working and the Kingdom growing?

The contrast between the in-your-face church on public display and the church hidden in local congregations is huge. I have friends who are mightily exercised over it (I just got a seven-page, single-spaced letter from one of them), but I feel like I can't even be bothered. There are enough of us who are simply doing our work, day in and day out: you and W____ and Linda in your congregations, me writing my books, and how many other thousands of anonymous others, that the church is in no danger of falling apart.

I used to be susceptible to the rhetoric of panic and alarm, but I seem to have developed a kind of bored nonchalance to the whole business. And you don't seem to be distraught. I don't want to become complacent and indifferent in this quiet and beautiful place of salvation perched over this lake. But neither do I want to be distracted—nor do I want my friends to be distracted—by the devil's public-relations pyrotechnics.

All the more reason that your sabbatical is timely—such a grace—to return you to your proper and strategic work in the trenches.

With much love and continuing prayer, Eric . . .

Dad

THE TWENTY-SIXTH LETTER

---

21 March

Lent 2006

Dear Eric,

The other day I was reflecting on my first years as
a pastor—getting the Christ Our King congregation
started—and thinking about the people/influences that
turned out to be formative. And remembered a poem
that I haven't read for years but has hung around the
edge of my awareness with some phrases that still mean
something. The poet is Philip Larkin, British, a self-
identified atheist, I think (although I've learned to hold
those professions of unbelief in a suspension of unbelief).
I'm enclosing the poem.

Those years I was trying hard not to fail, trying hard
to do this church/pastor thing right. I was immersed

in an adrenaline rush of being part of the Spirit's
creation of the miracles of church/congregation. I was
also immersed in the boosterism of church expansion
and church growth that seemed to have little interest
in anything past or lasting. The only phrase that
made any sense to me that I still remember is from an
older pastor who told me, "You are contemporary, but
nothing you do is temporary." Most of my advisors were
urging sociology on me, and relevance. I felt that they
were all trying to get me to use the tone and tactics of
used-car salesmen. And then I found this poem. I took
Philip Larkin into my congregation and sat him on a
back pew every Sunday (I don't think he would have
been comfortable any closer to the baptismal font).
And I tried to be his pastor—this detached outsider,
yet somehow attracted to what he doesn't understand,
"bored, uninformed . . ." And then this:

> It pleases me to stand in silence here;
> A serious house on serious earth it is,
> In whose blent air all our compulsions meet,
> Are recognised, and robed as destinies. . . .
> . . . someone will forever be surprising
> A hunger in himself to be more serious . . .[1]

I kept envisioning some bicyclist chancing by and
entering "in awkward reverence," and letting me be

his pastor.[2] Larkin provided me with a presence that
countered my own ego-adrenaline and the pushy
sales-force evangelism that was in vogue (and still is). I
kept Larkin as a companion, someone who might find
something that he didn't know he was looking for.
Find sanctuary, safe from the intrusions of priest or
pastor. A man or woman shy of religion as he or she had
encountered it; definitely not what is today designated
a *seeker*. Maybe I will write something someday with the
title "I Was Philip Larkin's Pastor."

I picked up George Eliot's novel *Adam Bede* the other
day and have been rereading it—amazed and delighted
by her wisdom and understanding of a church life and
spirituality that she did not embrace herself.[3] A Larkin-
like presence.

Your mother and I have been through a tough few
days. The director of the Lutheran camp fired the camp
manager a couple of weeks ago. Everybody we know in
the neighborhood and our church was totally bewildered,
some angry. Rick, the manager, is an amiable, joyful
man with incredible jack-of-all-trade skills, but with
some rough edges. (I think you've probably met him).
Perfect for this kind of job. Two young children that
all the campers fall in love with. We have become
close friends with him and his wife and children.
(His daughter, about seven or eight, tells her friends,

"Nu-gene is my best friend.") So yesterday, Jan and I asked to see Gary, the director. We both dreaded doing this, as he is also a friend.

I tried to establish common ground for the conversation by saying something on the order of "Gary, you and I are both pastors [he's an ordained Lutheran, but has been director of this camp for twenty-five years] and share responsibility for caring for the spiritual health of this community—and, as you know, the community is reeling right now—is there anything we can do to help you during this time of perplexity and bewilderment?" But it didn't work. He was cordial and inviting but spent the next hour or so talking like a camp director, not like a pastor. The big difficulty turns out to be that Rick has rough edges and sometimes offends people with his brusqueness; and he doesn't like the lists of jobs to do that Gary gives him—preferring to prioritize the work according to his on-the-job sense of what is next (the quality and amount of his work is not in question).

So for an hour we listened to Gary tell us why it is better for the camp to have Rick removed. And all the time, I am thinking, *Gary, you're a pastor: Pastors work with what they have.* "It is an ill mason that refuses any stone . . ." (George Herbert).[4] One of the upset neighbors and frequent volunteers at the camp in maintenance work said to me a couple of days ago, "If you have a horse that pulls his weight, and the horse farts, you don't put him down."

So we left feeling sad. There was nothing adversarial; everything was courteous and polite. But also the feeling that we occupied totally different worlds, and there was no common ground between us. For Gary, efficiency and public image trumps community.

The book on new-church development that was edited by Stanley Wood arrived, with the foreword that I wrote.[5] We talked about it. I'm sending you a couple of copies. Maybe it will be useful in the work you are doing with the presbytery on the new church development being planned.

Things are warming up here. We had probably our last day of cross-country skiing on Saturday. In a few weeks, we'll be swimming!

And how many days is it?[6]

The peace of our Lord,

Dad

THE TWENTY-SEVENTH
LETTER

———

29 May 2006

Dear Eric,

I don't know if this will get to you before you leave
on Thursday, but at least it will be there when you return
from your time at Christ in the Desert monastery. But
the little bit of time I had with you in Spokane on Friday
and Saturday got a conversation started that will have to
be written instead of spoken.

To begin with: an appreciation. You talk about
"coming out of the closet."[1] Which is fine. But I think
you have been very wise to cultivate and nurture your
own identity, your own *way* of being a pastor, with
as little interference from other people's identity
(including mine!), assumptions, or expectations as

possible. And it has worked. You have become more and more your unique, God-gifted self these years since your ordination. I have appreciated the continuity and congruence of our lives as father and son, and pastor and pastor, but I have absolutely delighted in the freshness and originality with which you have articulated and lived out your mature vocation. And now you are embarking on this sabbatical to make sure that you don't squander or dissipate the vocational skills and congregational intuitions and personal soul work that you have invested so much energy and prayer and love in becoming. I felt all of this while with you and reflected on it extensively on the drive home.

And I also reflected on the providential way that your involvement in the Institute for Christian Learning got me in on this Spokane gathering. I accepted the invitation because I know the group meant a lot to you, and also because my meeting with Nancy and Carl a few weeks ago seemed to confirm that we cared about the same things. But also that ICL was engaged in an aspect of congregation I have no skills in but is as necessary for the health of the church and its pastors as what I am doing and writing about. Everything that I had sensed and hoped might be true was confirmed in the Spokane conversations. The spirit, the language, the strategies, the people—I felt thoroughly at home and present with all of it.

In my offhand remarks at breakfast, I said that
I don't often use devil language but that it seems
appropriate in a setting like this: that a key strategy
of the devil in the present generation is to destroy
congregations. One obvious element in his strategy
seems to me to be to glamorize Big. Tempt every pastor
and congregation to admire and covet and build bigger
barns. As King Number is worshipped, baptismal
names erode into statistics. The very place given to
us by the Spirit where our stories can be known and
prayed and develop into a community story—a Kingdom
story—becomes the place where stories are destroyed
by programs, and particular people—especially the
marginal—are pushed deeper and deeper into anonymity.
Conversations get drowned out by motivational
propaganda. Relationships become depersonalized into
programmatic involvement with a vision or a cause. All
the time this is happening, the vocabulary and rhetoric
are entirely Christian, biblical, evangelical. The devil is
careful not to tamper with what is said or written; that
might set off an alarm among the heresy hunters. But
by destroying the congregation as congregation, the
congregations who fail to be Big languish in self-pity
or fester in envy, no longer able to see what the Spirit is
doing right there and then. And the congregations who
succeed in becoming Big, in the excitement of being part

of a winning "team" or organization, develop a huge case of amnesia regarding trivial, peripheral concerns like the cross of Jesus, the sacrificial life, the mystery of Resurrection, and "the least of these. . . ."[2] The Bible is no longer read as a text for living prayerfully and obediently—the full spectrum of the human condition and the staggering wonders of the revelation of God—but is advertised as the world's bestseller collection of bumper-sticker slogans, happy-face promises, and seven-step moralisms that can give you everything that is worth knowing in the Bible without having to bother reading it.

And then ICL shows up, and instead of fulminating against Big (like I do), quietly and skillfully gathers people together and shows them how to develop personal, relational organizations that work and give dignity to a people of God regardless of who and how many they are—free of intimidation. Anyway, that is what I came away from those gatherings with. I am glad that you got hooked up with them. And I am glad that I got in on a bit of involvement on the margin.

When I got home Saturday afternoon, Karen's birthday celebration was already going on under a full head of steam. Mary and Anna and Hans were providing enough energy to keep it going. Dave was there. Leif was just about ready to put the salmon on the grill: a new recipe of cooking with a tray of smoking alder

chips under the rack of salmon. Karen and Miles were
there: Miles entertained us later with three of his pastor/
congregation stories (quite excellent). Ray and Susie
Risho—a couple from Missoula who knew my mother
and had stayed in the old cabin thirty years ago, people
Karen admires and enjoys—who Karen wanted us to
invite and have stay overnight, were a delight. It was a
magnificent birthday dinner. Jan and I agreed that it
was the very best salmon that we had ever had: moist and
this gentle flavor of alder smoke. Karen seemed pleased,
said it was exactly what she had hoped it would be, which
pleased us. The only thing missing was you and your
family!

The countdown is over!

The peace of our Lord,

Dad

THE TWENTY-EIGHTH LETTER

—

6 September 2006

Dear Eric,

If I have my dates right, you returned to your pastoral
duties yesterday. I imagine you whistling and skipping
along with your dog, your coffee sloshing on the dog's
ears and over your shoes.

Your telephone report several days ago sounded so
wonderful as you described what you encountered in
terms of gratitude and insights and tears while hiking
the Wonderland Trail. Maybe that wouldn't (couldn't?)
have happened without two and a half months of
sabbatical behind you.

Sometimes I think if there is a one-answer solution
to recovering a mature and holy pastoral vocation in

America, it is to require that every congregation provide
a sabbatical every seven years. Even if half of the pastors
misuse or squander it, the net gain would have to be
extensive and profound. I just received a letter from
a Presbyterian pastor in Ireland who spent the first
ten days of his three-month sabbatical here with us
(mornings in conversation, afternoons driving around
the valley and Glacier), in which he recounted how
refreshed and full of energy he was, but that the most
important thing for both the congregation and himself
was the realization that he wasn't indispensable. (His
congregation is a little smaller than yours; he has been
there twenty-three years.)

I just got a good letter from Nancy Isaacson that
mentions you: "I have missed him. He is a new kind
of leader, I believe, who understands the undertow
of our time and culture on the human spirit and is
willing to structure his life in ways that keep him from
being sucked under. My paid work is full of being with
those who never see it, never know why they're short
of breath or vision, never question why they don't feel
wholehearted any more. Eric has an important role
to play, I think, in modeling how he goes about his
pastoring and his life."

I know that this sabbatical and the way you have
used it will have a major place in keeping you and your

congregation developing in a mature, focused, and Christ-centered way. Which is not easy.

I am preparing an address right now—mulling it over is more like it—and I think I want to make a point of what seems to me is characteristic in the American church today: namely, trivialization. Everything seems so trivialized. Fads spring up like mushrooms: seeker church, emergent church, megachurch, and on and on, and a lot more that I haven't heard of, I'm sure. Where are the pastors and congregations who just want to understand who and where they are, and study how to be faithful to who and where they are? I, in fact, know quite a few of them. And so do you. But there are so many others who show no evidence of being grounded. Because the world is in crisis, they think they have to fix the crisis. The consequence is that they fritter away their vocations and the gifts, needs, and opportunities that are right on their doorsteps. Have pastors ever been so bombarded by analyses of the culture and answers on how to package the gospel, to fix it? Maybe if they would all go into the wilderness for three months, not read their emails, announce a moratorium on all conventions and conferences, take a deep, long, prayerful time of doing nothing—maybe some equilibrium might return.

Dave and Ruthe Rugh were just here for seven days. We hadn't seen them for something like thirty-four

years. Cairn died a little over a year ago. They
were planning on coming last summer, but Ruthe
shattered her ankle, and it has been a slow and painful
convalescence. She still walks with a limp and a cane.
It was a good time to be with them. They (especially
Ruthe!) talked a lot about Cairn and the richness of
their life together for the nineteen years of her life.
As I listened to them, I simply marveled at what they
experienced and the way they experienced it. Cairn had
just about everything go wrong with her that is possible
in a human being. And they simply gave themselves
to her and each other, in every detail bringing out
the best in her, as she brought the best out of them.
Cheerful on both sides, Cairn and her parents patiently
weathered frequent life/death crises. Through all
this, they both worked full-time by negotiating special
hours so that one of them was always with Cairn. And
besides, they built their cedar home on the Olympic
Peninsula (not far from Port Townsend)—David doing
nearly all the carpentry and cabinetry. A beautifully
crafted piece of art.

One day as I was listening to them, this phrase—
frequent in the Hebrew Bible—came to mind: *niphlâ'oth*—
"wonders of the Lord." It is almost always used of things
like the Red Sea crossing, or miracles in the wilderness—
mighty acts of deliverance and salvation. But I had the

feeling that I was witnessing one of these *niphlâ'oth*, wondrous works, as it took place in the lives of Dave and Ruthe and Cairn, the three of them, *niphlâ'oth* brought about by the Spirit. That is not the kind of thing anyone can do with sheer willpower, not when it is suffused with such joy in every detail. In one sense, mountains and glaciers and oceans and sequoias—the kinds of things in creation that we marvel at (and the Hebrew Bible marvels at) are minuscule compared to what took place in these three, child/father/mother. And they are so unselfconscious about what they lived through and the life they celebrated so extravagantly. When this kind of thing takes place right before your eyes, it seems petty to bitch about what *isn't* going on in the church. And we have a ringside seat! Pastors get in on that quite often, don't you think?

They left on Monday. Karen came up and Leif/Amy and kids came for a cookout. Dave and Ruthe were able to be with us most of the day, and then left for a late flight back to Seattle. It seemed like a gift to have them with the rest of the family. Your family present would have made it a genuine, biblical *niphlâ'oth*!

The peace of our Lord,

Dad

THE TWENTY-NINTH LETTER

—

7 January 2007
The Baptism of Jesus

Dear Eric,

In worship this morning, W___ celebrated the
baptisms of 2006. Women had made banners, about two
feet square, with the name of the child baptized, and
they were draped over the communion rail. The maker of
the banner then presented it to the parents of the child,
saying, "I made this baptismal banner for [*name*]." And
then offered a prayer. Then the "rite of remembrance"
(enclosed) was prayed by the congregation. At each
baptism this year, Phyllis McCarthy (our best singer)
sang "I'm Going on a Journey" during the baptism.
And today the congregation sang it. Seven baptisms in
2006. In this octogenarian congregation of Abrahams

and Sarahs, Zechariahs and Elizabeths, this was quite something.

And, of course, I thought much of you and your pastoral baptismal focus, your sacramentally formed pastoral theology. I thought you would be pleased that at least one other pastor was making the most of this defining sacrament.

W____'s sermon wasn't the greatest, so I thought about you starting your preaching through Romans (which you announced in your newsletter). I think this is a fine thing to do, and you and your congregation are well enough acquainted by now to provide listening ears to this great letter. I preached through Romans at about the same number of years into my work with them. But I did it systematically—a chapter a week, sixteen sermons. I like the way you are doing it better, not overplanning but letting the text and congregation together provide the direction each week.

A few weeks ago, I wrote my Pentecostal friend (Foursquare) in Wenatchee. I was lamenting the loss, since Miles's retirement, of good baptismal stories (the big woman who fell on Miles in the baptistry, the old man in bib overalls who came up out of the water without the overalls and no underwear, etc.). Baptizing babies doesn't usually produce that much drama, at least not comic.

He responded with this, which I thought you might enjoy: "In good Arminian form, we dedicate babies instead of baptizing them. Seven or eight years ago, we all walked one of our fifteen-year-olds through pregnancy, childbirth, the finishing of high school, and eventually marriage. I got to do the ceremony in Snohomish, north of Seattle. She and her husband lived there but come back here to dedicate their babies. A few weeks ago, it was dedication number three.

"As I gathered the family in front of the church, the father began to hold little Mackenzie Jade in her special dress farther and farther from his body. I became aware of certain shiftings and whisperings that eventually became too animated to ignore. Uncrying, Mackenzie had exulted in the moment, offered all she could offer, filled her garments to pungent overflow like the oil down Aaron's robe. Nancy [Michael's wife] at the piano behind me and the family groups, said, 'Michael, we need a diaper.' Then, louder, 'Does anyone have a diaper?' In truth, we needed a pressure washer first. Another young father stood up from the crowd with a Huggies, and the parents went out to the nursery for several minutes.

"I had to tread water, trying to think of stories, etc. Finally, they came back, we prayed, thanked God for down-to-earthiness, laughter, incarnation, etc. As I dismissed the family, I said, 'You never know what's going to happen in church, whether it's going to be a baby dedication, a baby defecation, or both.'"

I wrote him back accusing him of abandoning Pentecostal eschatology and replacing it with a thoroughly unbaptized scatology.

As long as I can keep a few Pentecostal friends at hand, maybe the loss of Miles's stories won't be too impoverishing.

New Year's weekend we took Hans/Anna/Mary for two days while Leif and Amy had an overnight out with some of their friends, an annual event for them. They then joined us on New Year's Day for leg of lamb dinner. Nice. But on Sunday, after church, we took the kids to the Somers Cafe, a little, homey café where we occasionally have lunch. Two couples our age who we had just worshipped with were at the next table. As they left, they stopped and complimented the kids, exclaiming, "What precious children—and so well-behaved!" They overdid it a little, gushed. After they left, Hans said, "Grandpa, Grandma, we're not nearly as nice as they think we are." Which also is true.

I've been reading N. T. Wright the last few months. Three big books on the New Testament. I'm nearly done with the second, with the third waiting on the shelf. I've had them for four or five years but just got around to reading them this summer. I think there is a fourth, on Paul, on the way.[1] These books are absolutely magnificent. But they are long—each is seven to eight thousand pages. And so it takes forever to get through them. He deals with every last detail in the Gospel stories, fitting it into the Jewish world of the time and (against the Jesus Seminar people and others of their ilk) demonstrating the historical reasonableness of each detail when seen in its total context. I find him fascinating and enlarging. How one man can master so much material—and scholarly commentary and arguments—is beyond me. Staggering. I don't so much learn anything new, but he has the effect of making everything so much larger, more coherent. He has been a positive stimulus as I write my present spirituality book on Jesus' stories and prayers.

And here is another book I am liking a lot. Richard Lischer, *The End of Words*.[2] Do you know him? I met him once and liked him—a Lutheran, teaching at Duke. This is a really fine book on preaching—very congruent with what you do and the way you do it. I'd send you mine when I finish, but I accidentally knocked it into the toilet one morning, and so it is all waterlogged and warped (more scatological stuff!). I'll call you some day and see if you want it. If you do, I'll have a clean baptismal copy sent to you.

The cell phone that Karen gave us for Christmas is operational. On New Year's Day, Leif coached us through the technological maze. A few days later, Jan took it into town to her hair appointment and called me, just to make sure it worked. But she couldn't figure out how to do it, despite Leif's excellent lessons, and all the women in the beauty shop got into the act. It sounded like they were having a lot of fun (at our expense!).

So we are well launched into the new year. No guests this month, which is welcome. We are relishing the quiet. But it is interesting—we have a couple of men coming for several days in February, and already Jan is mentally/emotionally preparing, anticipating. And the writing is going well. I set myself a modest goal of writing five hundred words a day, and that is going really well. After those several months' moratorium on writing, I think I have the wind up again.

Your family picture is stunning.

With much love,

Dad

THE THIRTIETH LETTER

———

26 May 2007

Seventh Week of Easter

Dear Eric,

    I am making a new friend from the cemetery: Jacques
Maritain. I have had a lingering curiosity about him
for years. Used his phrase "purification of means" to
introduce *The Jesus Way*. But I have read only one book
of his, and that a long time ago. I picked up a couple
of books about him last summer when we were in Santa
Fe and have had them sitting on my shelf unread. A
few days ago, on impulse, I pulled one off and started
reading. Maybe Maritain kept himself out of my notice
until I was ready for him. But now I find myself so at
home in his company. Like having a conversation with
you—everything so congruent but expressed in such

personal ways out of such a local and lived context. I'm only twenty pages into the book, but as I began reading, I found myself deliberately slowing down, rereading sentences, shutting the book, and walking around outside.

One of the things that is immediately attractive is that his life in Christ was so intimately marital. He and his wife, Raïssa—both atheists—had decided together that if they couldn't find some meaning in life, they would commit suicide. Instead, they became Christians together and seemed to develop in holiness and maturity together. She wrote two volumes of memoirs that I have often seen mentioned, but never read. But I will now.

I love keeping company with him. He seems simply saturated with God. In comparison, I feel like I have my toes in the water. Every once in a while, a wave knocks me down and I'm temporarily saturated, sputtering and coughing, salt water up my nose. But I'm a long way from being out there in the deep, swimming with the whales. Even so, imperfect and erratic as life is, ankle deep at the edge of the ocean, I can't imagine going to one of those heated, chlorine-poisoned dinky pools that so many churches have installed in their sanctuaries.

The time with you in Alaska was so good. I keep remembering and appreciating and giving thanks for that time, the relationship. I felt that we were so integrated

and harmonious. So congruent. I'm glad that you are a
pastor, and I am glad that I have been close enough to
be in on your developing in your vocation and now going
full steam in your own unique maturity.

Today is your sister's birthday. Forty-seven years. A
birthday supper of shish kebab with Leif and Amy and
the grandkids, and Miles and Karen. It is a sunny day
(after a week of cold rain), and so we should be able to
cook and eat outside.

Here is a baptism story you can use in your pulpit next
Sunday. Two boys were wondering why nobody in the
neighborhood would play with them. They were shunned
by everyone. They came to the conclusion that it was
because they hadn't been baptized. So they went looking
for a church, found one, but the pastor wasn't there, only
the janitor. They asked him if he could baptize them.
"Sure." He took them into the bathroom, held each
one up in turn, holding him by the ankles, and dunked
his head in the toilet. As they left the church, they
talked about what kind of baptized Christian they were:
Catholic? No, they just sprinkle some water on your head.
Baptist? No, they nearly drown you. "I know," said one.
"Did you smell that water? We're E-piss-copalians!"

The water is fast coming up in the lake—a couple of
feet from full pool. Did I tell you that Miles has done
the repair work from last summer's storm? And the rock

work where the storm tore out part of the understructure
of the patio. A fine job, cementing in stones to make
steps to the right of the dock, and making a shallow
wading pool on the left.

I keep reflecting on our time in Alaska. The agony
of Steve and Janet, the confusion in the congregation.
I don't know which is harder these days: to be a pastor
or to be a congregation. This morning I read in my
Maritain book how as he was thinking and reading and
talking about becoming a Christian (Catholic), it was
like digging through a dunghill to find a precious stone.[1]

Did I tell you that Jeffrey W. has become a Catholic?
He has been talking about it for years, as you know.
But now he has done it. He has concluded that he
has no vocation to be a pastor or a priest. He has an
appointment as professor of philosophy at a Catholic
college in Emmitsburg (Mount St. Mary's) beginning in
September. Meanwhile, he is finishing up his dissertation
at Catholic University. He has notified the presbytery of
his decision. He seems relieved, having made the decision.
I hope it holds. I think, knowing Jeffrey, that I can
understand it. But I can't help but wonder if he will find
things any better as a Catholic. Church is church under
whatever name. A dunghill. And Presbyterian dung and
Catholic dung are about as different as cow dung and
horse dung. But there is treasure in that dunghill, as you

and I both know. But there are so many who never find
the gems. Do they give up too soon? Are they looking
for the wrong thing?

A United Church of Christ pastor came here three
weeks ago. A year ago, he had arranged to start out
his sabbatical by coming here from Pennsylvania (near
Gettysburg). He asked for twice-daily, one-hour
conversations for three weeks. Came with his wife. They
are both fifty-six, married for five years, both widowed.
The first week was a little stiff, but then everything
opened up, and we had fine conversations. He has
evolved from a Baptist upbringing to a very pastor-
personal style structured in a Eucharistic liturgy. He has
been patient and gone about it slowly but seems content
to work with his people as long as they are willing. And
they seem quite willing. He confirms my conviction
that with enough love and sacrifice and focus, most
congregations are capable of learning how to worship
and be led into a mature life. The last day here, Jan fixed
a crab quiche, and both of them came to supper for a
concluding conversation. It was good to have them in a
setting of hospitality with both of them in it together. I
like doing this kind of thing.

I am putting a small book in the mail to you, *The
Shack*.² Did I mention this to you in Juneau? It was sent in
manuscript to me by the publisher of a small outfit. He is

an old acquaintance, asking me for an endorsement. It is not a perfect book, but I found it absolutely fascinating. Your mother and I read it together aloud. A tragedy forms the plotline, but the story develops an exposition of the Trinity that I found stunningly imaginative and, I think, accurate. I know nothing about the author—a first novel.

We are looking forward to Drew's graduation. As you know, I won't get there for the ceremony but will get in on the festivities. Can't wait.

The peace of our Lord,

Dad

THE THIRTY-FIRST LETTER

---

31 August 2007

Fourteenth Week in Pentecost (I think)

Dear Eric,

A rough forest-fire season. For three weeks, we didn't see the mountains across the lake or the sun, moon, and stars in the sky. Ash and cinders all over the deck each morning, some of it seeping into the house, although we kept the windows shut. We seriously thought we were LEFT BEHIND and began searching through the experts on these things for a loophole. And then a week ago, suddenly the skies opened and we saw blue skies—a visible heaven. We cancelled the midnight apocalypse prayer meetings.

Karen, my sister, is having a difficult time with her body. She has excruciating pain in her back—apparently

a nerve caught in a vertebrae, although the diagnosis
is not certain. This has been going on for two to three
months. She tries everything: acupuncture, craniosacral,
chiropractic, organic diet, the pain clinic, conventional
doctor. And, of course, painkillers and steroid injections.
She is frantic, and on the edge of slipping into a scary
depression, which almost did her in twenty years ago.
Everyone feels helpless. There doesn't seem to be
anyone in the medical world who more or less steps
forward and takes charge. I go over each Saturday
afternoon and bring her and Miles the Eucharist and
anointing oil (in the little vial you gave me), hoping
that with that in place, not depending on her condition
or level of need, I will introduce something objectively
sacramental into her life. Kevin and Karen and kids were
here last week; Kim and C. C. and kids are here this
week. Despite, or maybe because of, the activity and
grandkids and care, she feels increasingly isolated. She
has an appointment at the pain clinic for a procedure a
week from today. For which, I fear, she has far too much
(desperate) expectation.

Their pastor (the church in Bigfork) is no pastor.
Never calls or visits. Miles said the other day, "I don't
think there are any pastors anymore." This guy is into
"vision casting."

A woman from Christ Our King called yesterday and kept me on the phone for an hour. I was her pastor for twenty-five years—I think she may have taught you in Sunday school, Ellie Deane. She is seventy-five years old. Faithful at Christ Our King all these years, loves Pastor Linda, loves the worship and community. But she has been watching Sister Angelica on TV (a Catholic channel) and is absolutely smitten by her. Says the rosary with Sister A. every night in front of the TV. Is intoxicated with the celebrity Catholics that parade across the screen. She wants to convert. I tried to listen sympathetically, tried my best to affirm her. Tried to understand what was going on. And assured her that it would be ok with the HS whether she was at St. Mark's or Christ Our King. But then I said, "Ellie, you realize, don't you, that if you convert to an RC, you will never have a pastor again? Priests are vastly overworked and don't make pastoral calls. That is not a priority with them. When you get sick and are dying, it is very unlikely that you will have a priest caring for you. If you are lucky, he will show up for the last rites."

She said, "Well, they have deacons to do that." And then she added that the deaconess with whom she has been talking is upset because of Benedict's reinstitution of the Tridentine Mass in Latin, and deacons and deaconesses will no longer be permitted to give the Eucharist. She has never been to Mass.

I observed that everything she knew about Catholicism was through a television screen—spiritual stars that she never talks to, knows nothing about, and who know nothing about her. "Is that the world you want to inhabit?" She had never thought of that.[1]

Maybe she needs to convert. I like her very much. She is widowed—I knew the family quite intimately during the Christ Our King years. But I wonder how much this is just sheer romance, romantic spirituality. Oprah in nun's clothing.

Jeffrey W. told me that, during the presbytery meeting in which he was released from his ordination to become a Catholic, three congregations also left to join up with a purer form of church. People jumping off both sides of the ship.

Meanwhile, I am also in touch with a lot of men and women who are content to be modest Christians and faithful pastors. And I know you are too. The remnant seems pretty solid. It always is.

But anything I can do in the years I have left to present and reinforce in what I am writing to recover a solid, Trinitarian, baptism-grounded ecclesiology, I want to do.

We have had a series of guest cancellations that were disappointing, but then, to our surprise, energizing. We love having these friends, but it is also nice to have some space and time to just be ourselves: Jerry Sittser cancelled because of a furnace problem; Sister Constance cancelled a weeklong visit because of the air pollution; Murray Pura and family cancelled because of illness; Paul and Gail Stevens and John and Lillian Toews from Vancouver cancelled because of surgeries.

I finished my fourth volume this week, *Tell It Slant.* We had guests the next day. Tom (his family having supper with us), after serving ten years with World Concern in Kenya, and an accomplished computer user, offered to send the mss electronically to our agent (I had said I didn't know how to do it). So he did. The next day I called to see if everything had gone all right; it hadn't. Everything was gibberish. And then my flash SanDisk[2] only showed half the mss on it. I panicked. But then everything was recovered through a different conversion program, and so it is now safe in the arms of Eerdmans. In the process of fooling around with the email stuff, I found a message from you dating from a couple of weeks ago. I made a pre-New Year resolution: Eugene, learn how to work this email world of technology!

Between the fire and brimstone, Karen's medical trials, ecclesiastical defections, email gibberish, and disappearing guests, I feel apocalyptic. Maybe it's time to read the Revelation again!

I didn't intend, when I sat down to write this morning, to construct a litany quite like this. But there it is. These are the times I really miss being in a congregation where everything is organic, rooted in worship, where I am in personal, tactile, and auditory relation with the well and the sick, the sin and the sanctity in a liturgical rhythm that keeps everything in salvation mode. Like you are.

The peace of our Lord,

Dad

THE THIRTY-SECOND LETTER

------

19 November 2007

Dear Eric,

It's a rainy Saturday. I completed a chapter of my
Ephesians manuscript, *Practice Resurrection: A Conversation
on Growing Up in Christ*. I don't know how much I have told
you about this since you heard the first four chapters at
Whitworth this summer. Today I completed the seventh
chapter. I'm halfway through. I hope I can complete
the manuscript by May. I think I can, due to saying no
to virtually every invitation I have received for the next
two years. It feels good to have these blank spaces on the
calendar.

Yesterday I was in Polson for a presbytery meeting.
They invited me to address them for an hour and a

half. I talked for about forty minutes, and then there was discussion for another forty. It went okay. It was a friendly congregation. But I also felt a little dull; I talked about the church and some of the themes in Ephesians, but I was tired, and the spark wasn't there. I hope they weren't too disappointed.

In this business of Ephesians and church, I feel more exposed somehow to the indifference and hostility of the American church—but not yesterday at presbytery. I often feel that I am going against the stream in what I am writing, that in this area of church and congregation, there is a torrent that I am swimming against. And I have to fight against the feeling of futility—of being summarily dismissed by all the people I want to address— pastors, mostly, but also that whole parachurch crowd who have little use for the church except when they can use it for their promotion and get money from it.

Except for a few rare intermissions. The time with you at Colbert was one of those. You do that so well— understand the church from the inside, take church seriously as *church*. And every time we are there, your mother and I feel truly blessed—blessed, *lucky*. We feel we are at the center of health and sanctity and maturity. And I know there are many other congregations and pastors who are doing it with skill and sanctity too. I just don't happen to be around very often when it is happening.

But here is something that fortifies hope. In rustling through some unfiled papers, I came across a letter from maybe fourteen years ago from Louise Wheatley. You might not remember her. She came to church at the invitation of some twelve-step friends—her husband is an alcoholic and her son a serious drug addict. She kept coming, and in a few months had become a Christian, and I became her pastor. She was absolutely new to all this. Had never been to church, was raised in a decent and stable family. But no religion. God was not a part of their working vocabulary. Louise is an artist, quite accomplished, works in textiles. And keeps up an active relationship with a number of artist friends. After about four years of being her pastor, we left to go to Vancouver. Letters replaced voiced conversations. Here is the letter that I received from her that I just found that I think is so quintessentially *Louise*, but also exhibit A on the nature of church.

> *Dear Pastor:*
>
> Among my artist friends I feel so defensive about my life, I mean about going to church. They have no idea what I am doing and act bewildered. So I try to be unobtrusive about it. But as my church life takes on more and more importance—it is

essential now to my survival—it is hard to
shield it from my friends. I feel protective
of it, not wanting it to be dismissed or
minimized or trivialized. It is like I am
trying to protect it from profanation
or sacrilege. But it is so strong that it is
increasingly difficult to keep it quiet. It is
not as if I am ashamed or embarrassed—I
just don't want it belittled. A longtime
secular friend, and a superb artist, just the
other day was appalled: "What is this I
hear about you going to church?" Another
found out that I was going on a three-week
mission to Haiti and was incredulous: "You,
Louise, you going to Haiti with a church
group. What has gotten into you?" I don't
feel strong enough to defend my actions.
My friends would accept me far more
readily if they found that I was in some
bizarre cult involving exotic and strange
activities like black magic or experiments in
levitation. But going to church is branded
with a terrible ordinariness. But that is
what endears it to me, both the church
and the twelve-step meetings—this facade
of ordinariness. When you pull back the

veil of ordinariness, you find the most
extraordinary life behind it. But I feel
isolated and inadequate to explain to my
husband and close friends—even myself!—
what it is. It's as if I would have to undress
myself before them. Maybe if I was willing
to do that, they would not dare disdain me.
More likely, they would just pity me. As it is,
they just adjust their neckties a little tighter.
I am feeling raw and cold and vulnerable
and something of a fool. I guess I don't
feel too badly about being a fool within the
context of the secular world. From the place
from which they look at me, I don't have
much to show for my new life. I can't point
to a life mended. Many of the sorrows and
difficulties seem mended for a time only to
bust open again. But to tell you the truth, I
haven't been on medication since June, and
for that, I feel grateful.

When I try to explain myself to these
friends, I feel as if I am suspended in a hang
glider between the material and immaterial,
casting a shadow down far below, and they say,
"See, it's nothing but shadow work." Perhaps
it takes a fool to savor the joy of shadow work,

the shadow cast as I am attending to the
unknown, the unpaid for, the freely given.

That's the letter.

From somebody who is totally unschooled in church
and knows nothing of the Bible until recently, that letter
seems to me a gem. She has no romantic illusions about
church. She knows that she can't defend or explain it to
the satisfaction of her friends. Nobody has any idea of
what she is doing, and she feels apologetic about that.
But she has embraced what she is given—that seemingly
fragile hang-glider church suspending her in the
mystery—in her words, "the unpaid for, the freely given."
She is there. She could not *not* be there. She didn't expect
to find nice people, people of accomplishment, artists.
But she is an artist in matters of church: "Don't look
at me—see the shadow down there. Look at the shadow
work. You might see what God is doing." She knows so
little about the church, but she knows what it is. With an
artist's intuition, she perceives the energy that keeps the
ligaments and sinews and fabric of the hang glider that
she is strapped into, a seemingly fragile church that casts
on the earth what she calls *shadow work*.

She is still in it, still hang gliding. She has been out
here to see us a couple of times. But I had forgotten all
about that letter until I just found it.

I think I got a little carried away just now with Louise.
Maybe I can find a way to work that into my manuscript.

Here's another church story, this one not so glorious.
Jeff Teeples is an associate pastor at Christ Lutheran
in Whitefish, has been there ten years. He and his wife,
Kris, have been coming to see Jan and me every month
for eight years. Recently things turned sour at the
church. The pastor is a very impersonal, ambitious man
who launched the church (*bullied* the church was more
like it) into a five-million-dollar building project. It
is not going well. I know him quite well. He has come
to me twice asking for money (which he didn't get).
He is under the gun from all sides. He moved into a
take-charge, pushy leadership style of efficiency and
productivity. He fired Kris, who was on the church staff,
made Jeff account for every hour on the job, submitting
weekly accounts which he examines and critiques. It
became intolerable, and so Jeff went to the bishop and
said he needed to leave. It took only six weeks to get
a call to a church in Minnesota as senior pastor in a
healthy church.

But here's the hitch. This is their last Sunday. Pastor
John planned to provide a farewell ceremony after
church this Sunday, in which there would be laying on
of hands and appreciative comments from the leadership.
Kris refuses to do it—Pastor John has not spoken to her

since he fired her. Jeff doesn't want to do it—feels that John is just providing a smoke screen of appreciation. So Jeff asked me if I would come and give the prayer of blessing. I said I would if Pastor John would personally invite me. I didn't think he would—but he did. So we are going tomorrow. I'll do my best. But the church is disintegrating, even as I am preparing to do it.

Karen and Miles are in Seattle, trying to get some medical help—things haven't gone well at all with the doctors here.

Hans's birthday is Monday—wants to come here for supper. Has ordered macaroni and cheese with hamburger and peas. We'll feast in the style of Clark House cuisine.

Sorry for the ramble . . . I needed some pastor talk!

Love you Eric!

Dad

THE THIRTY-THIRD LETTER

---

5 January 2008

Dear Eric,

Betty's memorial service, "the completion of her
baptism" (I have come to love that phrase as I have
heard you use it), was today. Your mother and I have
participated in both the grief and celebration. We are
so grateful that you have had such a person in your life,
particularly in these foundation years of the church's life.

In some ways I envy you in having a praying, mature,
always-in-the-background person like Betty. Never
self-conscious about her "leadership gifts," never
asserting herself. Her presence in the congregation, I am
imagining, provided a living model for what it means to
live as the body (not the head!) of the church. I never had

anybody like that. I didn't know there were people like that around and so never missed it. But in retrospect, I miss it.

I am sorry that you weren't able to get to Chicago before she died. Jan and I talked about the many times that happened to us. Every time that happened, I felt gypped, not being present. We were away at the deaths of Charla Bryant, George Moore, Edmund Scarborough, Chloe Brown (Edith Brown's granddaughter's crib death), Cathy Stewart . . . All people we knew well and had shared in a lot of prayer and worship and nitty-gritty living.

Karen and Miles returned on Monday after eight weeks in Seattle. We are having a difficult time discerning just what is appropriate for us to do. In their absence, we realized how much emotional energy has been draining out of us over this past year. Karen's steadily deteriorating spinal condition and the steadily increasing pain. The frantic effort to get medical help and the accumulation of disappointments on that front. As the days approached for their return, we found ourselves apprehensive. For the last several months, Jan has prepared a lot of meals for them. She has resumed that in this week of their return. It takes its toll. And we don't want to get mired in it. But what do we do when this is taking place next door? Miles is magnificent in his attentiveness and patience, but it is wearing him down. And he is no help with meals—he doesn't have a clue in meal preparation. So we talk and pray and wait for discerning wisdom.

Thanks for your Christmas gifts. The gloves, besides being warm, are classy. Jan gave me a pocket watch since my other one expired a few months ago. So I'm keeping with the times.

The peace of our Lord . . . and much love,

Dad

THE THIRTY-FOURTH LETTER

———

1 February 2008

Hi Eric . . . Happy Birthday!

Another lap around the track . . . another mountain
peak climbed . . . another turn of the crank . . . another
candle in the cake . . . another notch in the gun stock . . .
How many ways are there to memorialize a birthday?

But did we ever tell you this? When we were driving
you home after your birth at Union Memorial Hospital
in Baltimore, I noticed that I was being followed by a
state patrol car but didn't think much about it. Actually
I felt pretty good about it, having a police escort on the
hazardous stretch of road up Route 1. I was intent on
getting you home safe and sound and was well under
the speed limit and keeping all the rules. But when we
turned onto Saratoga Drive, the patrol car turned in

after me and immediately set off his siren. I pulled over. The officer came up and told me that I was driving with New York license plates past the legal four-month limit for getting Maryland tags. Apparently I had been under police surveillance all that time. I was a week past the deadline. I explained to the officer that it was all because of you. Your mother held you up so he could get a good look. He was impressed. He took one look at you and agreed that that was about the best reason for breaking the law he knew of. He didn't give me a ticket. I thanked him for the police escort to your new home. I think he was proud that he had done it.

And we have been proud ever since. All these birthdays. This rich accumulation of memories. And now, today, a deep appreciation for your life and the way you have lived your life. The many, many ways in which you have honored your mother and me. The wisdom and love that you have exercised so lavishly as spouse and parent. The skilled and generous ways you have lived the pastoral vocation. The prayerful and thoughtful ways in which you have lived your baptismal identity.

So whatever it is for you, your birth was and is and continues to be a happy birthday for your mother and me.

Thanks.

Dad

THE THIRTY-FIFTH LETTER

—

Dear Eric,

Two days ago, spring finally arrived. Yesterday
everything was happening—birds everywhere,
wildflowers opening like firecrackers under our
feet, the lake rising. I wrote in the morning, but
all afternoon we spent outside, putting the summer
cushions out on our summer furniture, cleaning flower
beds, weed-eating the grass at the entrance. Earlier, I
had stacked the wood you cut up while you were here.
Miles cut down that dead tree that was leaning out—
didn't quite get it to fall where he aimed it, and so it
took a gouge out of the dock, but not bad. So things
are getting shipshape.

Friday evening we had a first, the First Annual Hughes Bay Progressive Dinner: We started out at John and Joan Greene's for appetizers, a large, very attractive home around the point south, full of original art and mounted trophies on most walls from John's African safaris (John is a neurosurgeon from Nebraska, where he obviously made it big!); then to John and Kelly Swenson's, a very tasteful log home just east of the Sauers facing the Lutheran camp, for the main course (the Swensons organized the event); and dessert at our place. About twenty people participated, some we hardly knew. It was very congenial, interesting conversations, affable—it turned out that we all liked one another! We rarely see one another day by day. So this was very welcome. And timely, just before summer and its heightened activity kicks in. Everybody wants to keep it going.

We basked in the afterglow of our Mother's Day/Pentecost days with you on our drive home, conversationally savored the time with you and your kids, to say nothing of the congregation. A blessed congregation, truly. And pleased at how smooth the congregational meeting went.

Our friends Wade and Carol Mason took us morel-mushroom hunting three years ago and invited us again. Tomorrow morning. We had a humdinger of a forest fire last year northwest of Kalispell near Tally Lake, and that

creates favorable conditions for a harvest of morels. So
we leave early in the morning to see what we can find.

I think I have found a rhythm and "voice" for
my memoir. Have forty or so pages now, and think I
know what I want to do. I think I told you that I had
considerable anxiety about this while anticipating it. I
have never written in this style before. I have always had
a text. This seems so much more exposed and chancy.
But I didn't want to ask for advice either. I didn't want
to be working under someone else's idea of who I was or
the way I should do it.

When Rick proposed that I write this (did I tell you
this?), he got two publishing houses interested in it. One
of them sent three executives out here to get me to sign
with them, and Rick joined us. They were very pushy,
told me exactly what I needed to do, had the "best
editor for memoirs in the business." They were in our
living room for three hours and made their pitch—and
offered a huge advance. They never asked me anything.
Never made any attempt to get to know your mother or
me. There was a kind of arrogance that went with their
awareness that they were the biggest Christian publisher
in the business and knew how to make this a bestseller.
We felt crowded in our own living room—it was all
business but disguised, of course, as "ministry." When
we were in NYC a couple of years ago for an alumni

event with my old seminary, we had lunch with the editor and publisher of Viking Press in a little restaurant in Greenwich Village. Two women, both Christians (one Catholic and one Lutheran, we eventually learned), but quiet about it. They were relaxed and easy, spent a couple of hours in conversation, got to know us as we got to know them. There was no mention of a memoir—just getting to know one another. Later they made an offer of an advance to Rick that was half of what was previously proposed. When Rick tried to get them to raise it, they demurred. But there was no question about our decision—Viking, hands down. I know Rick was disappointed. When the publishers learned of our decision, they were furious—called Rick and demanded an explanation—and raised their advance. Rick is good at this kind of thing. He was honest with them, told them that they had "taken over" our space and crowded us out of our own living room and that Viking had given us the dignity of not responding to an evangelical sales pitch.

I have less and less tolerance for Evangelicals (with a big *E*). I'm so glad that you have been able to develop a congregation that is thoroughly evangelical without buying into the Evangelical subculture. And that you have that kind of support and affirmation from Bill Robinson and the Whitworth ethos. (I haven't read his mss yet but will this week.)

But having said that, I think after another thirty pages or more, to make sure that I have a feel for what I am able to do and want to do, I will submit what I have done so far, sixty or seventy pages, to Carolyn, my Viking editor, for a reality check. I have a deadline of June 15, 2009—if I am way off base, I will have time to revise my approach (if I can) or return the advance.

Hope your retreat at the monastery went well. I'm glad that you have learned how to be what Moomaw names a lazy pastor. He has probably never heard the word *contemplative.*

With steadfast love and the peace of our Lord,

Dad

THE THIRTY-SIXTH LETTER

———

21 July 2008

Dear Eric,

I keep reflecting on the pleasure I continue to experience from doing the foreword with you for Bill's book,[1] maybe especially because it was almost entirely your work and I felt so included. I know that I cannot take this kind of thing for granted, to sense this congruence between our lives at this time in our lives, you in your midlife, me in my concluding years.

I have been rereading a collection of Barth's correspondence, beginning with the letters he wrote after his visit to America in the early 1960s.[2] Jan and I heard him lecture at Princeton when he was here—it was just before we came to Bel Air. He was seventy-five years old and had just retired from his post in Basel.

He uses the phrase several times in these letters of his "dishonorable discharge" from his professorship in Basel. I had forgotten the details, but also forgotten how much it bothered him. The faculty at Basel had unanimously, with Barth's approval, nominated his successor (Gollwitzer). The university ignored their wishes and appointed someone (Heinrich Ott) who would set out on a very different way of doing theology, a way without sympathy or continuity with Barth. I don't know the details, but Barth used phrases like "an unholy stink" surrounding the political maneuverings, his own "isolation," and said that in his meetings with his twelve or so doctoral students, he didn't have access to the university buildings but had to meet either in a nearby restaurant or in his home.

It seems so sad—to be honored as a great, probably definitive theologian of the twentieth century—and feeling "dishonorably discharged" from the university that he had just retired from. And here I am, also seventy-five years old, and I know that you are carrying on a life both personal in your family and vocational as a pastor that gives me such feelings of continuity and pleasure. I never felt as if you were doing it to please me. You certainly never copied me. You have done it in a way that is true to who you are. And in a way that I can take immense pleasure in. I feel so fortunate. Thank you.

I am toiling away at the memoir and feeling more confident. The one thing that I want to avoid, if at all possible, is any suggestion that I am any kind of model for an American pastor. I am convinced that the pastoral vocation is the most context-specific vocation there is: the pastor's emotional life, experience in the church, aptitudes, and working this all out in an actual congregation, these people, at this time in history and culture. No copying. No trying to be successful. But how do I do that without coming across as someone who has done it "right" that anyone else can use as a blueprint? No two pastors are alike—maybe just like no two marriages are alike. The ways in which the vocation of pastor is conceived and develops and comes to birth are unique to each pastor.

So what do I hope for? I am trying to get this clear in my imagination—writing to you right now is trying to "get it clear." I am aware, of course, that there is a great deal of confusion in North America about pastoral identity. Many pastors, disappointed or disillusioned with congregations, defect after a few years and find more congenial work. And many congregations, disappointed or disillusioned with their pastors, dismiss them and look for a pastor more to their liking. If I'm not mistaken, these defections and dismissals have reached epidemic proportions. I keep thinking that it might be useful to somehow use this memoir to be in conversation with both pastors and people who have pastors.

I wonder if at the root of much of the "defection and dismissal" business isn't a kind of cultural assumption that leaders are people who "get things done" and "make things happen." That is certainly true of the primary leadership models that seep into celebrities and athletes. But while being a pastor certainly has some of those components, the pervasive element in our two-thousand-year pastoral tradition is not as someone who "gets things done" but someone who pays attention to "what is going on right now" between men and women, with each other and with God. Something that is primarily local and relentlessly personal.

I don't want to mount a polemic or criticize the secular-leadership models but simply give witness to another way of understanding "pastor." A way that can't be measured or counted and often isn't even noticed.

I think I would like to provide dignity to this very modest and often obscure way of life, pastor, in the Kingdom of God.

The men and women who are pastors today have entered into a way of life in which two thousand years of practice and tradition are in ruins. Continuities with our

ancestors are virtually nonexistent. We are a generation
that feels like it has to start from scratch to represent
and nurture the richly nuanced and all-involving life of
Christ to a generation "which knew not Joseph."[3] Faced
with this cultural condition, the vocation of pastor is
being scrapped by many and replaced by strategies of
religious entrepreneurism. I have no criticism of that
(well, maybe a little!), but I would like to validate the far
more modest vocation of pastor. We don't hold the most
important position in Kingdom work, but we are not
obsolete. Not by a long shot.

Remember the Anne Tyler novel *Saint Maybe*?[4] Maybe.
Would that be a good modifier to set alongside pastor?
Pastor Maybe? Would "maybe" serve as a disclaimer
to expertise and at the same time a reminder of the
ambiguity always involved in the vocation? Pastor Maybe:
Given the loss of a cultural or ecclesial consensus on how
to go about this, none of us are sure of what we are doing
as pastors, only *maybe*. William Faulkner was once asked
how he went about writing a book. "You grab any board
or shingle flying by or loose on the ground and nail it
down fast."

Most of the pastors that I know well and respect
experience a good deal of tentativeness in much of what
they do. Would a memoir provide a congenial form to
bring that out into the light of day?

But would anybody buy a book with the title *Pastor Maybe?*

You don't have to respond to any of this—I just needed someone who knows what I have been doing to work out this stuff with on paper. I'll keep at it.

We'll be seeing you in a little over a week!

Your dad, with love,

Dad

THE THIRTY-SEVENTH LETTER

---

21 June 2010

Dear Eric,

Yesterday was such a focus and time of gratitude for
your mother and me. After we left Karen in Missoula
yesterday afternoon, for the two hours on our drive
home, we talked of the deeply textured experience
of the day with you and your children on that double
celebration, your twentieth anniversary of ordination
and Father's Day with your children and us.

But I needed a letter—maybe something more like a
Timothy Letter—to work out some of the reflections that
surfaced in our conversation as we returned here, driving
north under the shadow of our splendid mountains. The
emails of the last two years have been wonderful. They

were just the right thing to keep us connected with all
the day-by-day pain and trauma involved in that descent
into hell. But this morning, I need a more reflective
medium to express what is going on right now, both past
and present and which includes so much of our shared
lives.

Psalm 21 for a start. As I said yesterday to the
congregation, I had been looking for two or three weeks
for a word from Scripture that might give a focus on what
we were doing. And then on Saturday evening, browsing
through my Bible at the Clark House, there it was. The
word that hooked me in the psalm was *bless*: "You bestow
on him blessings forever."[1] You wrote to me after you had
spent those several days of retreat (was it in Indiana?)
after writing that long meditation on where you were
and what was going on in your life (*our* lives) right then,
something on the order of "I am a man of blessing. . . ."
That seemed to me magnificently extraordinary but not
in any way forced or contrived. It seemed to be the most
biblical and accurate word there is to state the reality of
your life. And still does.

This was reinforced in detail after worship as so many
people came to me and expressed appreciation for you
as their pastor. They always do this when we are there,
but there was a lot more of it yesterday. A statement
from one woman struck me as perceptive but also

characteristic. She said, "I love the way his preaching is so contemplative—he pauses, lets some silence develop, as if waiting (praying?) for the right word—and then it is there, it *is* the right word."

And then, the bonus of a Father's Day meal together with your children. That was unexpected. And what are the chances of that taking place impromptu like that? As we drove to the restaurant, Sadie was more talkative than usual. She learned that Jan was trained as a teacher and taught the first year of our marriage. She said, "I am going to be a teacher, and teach first grade." And then she began elaborating parallels with Jan—"we both skipped second grade, we both are the third child, and teaching first grade is part of our lives." She was genuinely animated. It was delightful to listen to her include herself in that way with her grandmother.

And I think I mentioned this to you yesterday. As we were trying to be unnoticed and inconspicuous in the parking lot, Elizabeth parked beside us and immediately recognized us. We hastened to vow her to silence. So she was part of the "secret" before anyone else knew anything. I also thought that was a gift.

As your mother and I are increasingly aware these days that we are in the process of, as you would say, completing our baptisms both vocationally and parentally, yesterday was such a gift of experiencing the deep, deep, continuities that are so energetically apparent in the three generations on display in your congregation and family. We returned home rejoicing. Thank you. We love you.

The peace of our Lord,

Dad

NOTES

INTRODUCTION

1. Eugene H. Peterson, *Run with the Horses: The Quest for Life at Its Best*, commemorative ed. (Downers Grove, IL: IVP Books, 2019).
2. 1 Timothy 1:2, NIV.
3. Franz Kappus, introduction to *Letters to a Young Poet* by Rainer Maria Rilke (Novato, CA: New World Library, 2000), 5.

THE FIRST LETTER

1. Melody was a music director at Colbert Presbyterian Church.
2. Lynn was Eric's first wife. She was involved in Colbert Presbyterian Church when the church was first formed.

THE SECOND LETTER

1. The series of lectures here referenced as "Follow the Leader" was eventually published as *The Jesus Way: A Conversation on the Ways That Jesus Is the Way* (Grand Rapids, MI: Eerdmans, 2011).

THE THIRD LETTER

1. Eugene's reflections in these letters occasionally made their way into his later books. A few paragraphs here would eventually be adapted for his memoir *The Pastor: A Memoir* (San Francisco: HarperOne, 2011), 315.
2. Psalm 40:4.

THE FOURTH LETTER

1. By "Search," Eugene is perhaps referring to the Center for Organizational Reform (COR), a ministry (now defunct) that helped individuals and

institutions pursue health and resilience. Both Eugene and I did work for COR over the years.

2. Eugene revisits this story of John Henry Newman in his memoir *The Pastor* (page 225).

THE FIFTH LETTER

1. Eugene may have picked up this quotation from Dorotheus of Gaza from Kathleen Norris's book *Amazing Grace: A Vocabulary of Faith* (New York: Riverhead, 1999), 32. Norris doesn't cite it. Eugene was pretty fluent in patristic literature, so he may have quoted from a primary source.

THE SIXTH LETTER

1. James Michener, *The Source: A Novel* (New York: Dial Press, 2014).
2. Isaiah 34:13; 35:7, KJV.

THE SEVENTH LETTER

1. *SPU*: Seattle Pacific University.

THE NINTH LETTER

1. Wendell Berry, "Manifesto: The Mad Farmer Liberation Front," accessed September 20, 2019, https://cals.arizona.edu/~steidl/Liberation.html.
2. Thomas Lynch, *The Undertaking: Life Studies from the Dismal Trade* (New York: Penguin, 1997).
3. Thomas Lynch, *Bodies in Motion and at Rest: On Metaphor and Mortality* (New York: W. W. Norton, 2000).
4. *Some doubted*: Matthew 28:17; *went back to fishing*: John 21:1-14; *three-hour walk to Emmaus*: Luke 24:13-35.

THE TENTH LETTER

1. Audio for these talks is included in *Creation and Gospel: From the Garden to the Ends of the Earth*, available from the Regent College bookstore.

THE THIRTEENTH LETTER

1. 1 John 3:2. Eugene is paraphrasing here, probably from memory.

THE SIXTEENTH LETTER

1. Lynn was a music director for Colbert Presbyterian Church.
2. This letter appears in Eric E. Peterson, *Letters to a Young Congregation: Nurturing the Growth of a Faithful Church* (Colorado Springs, CO: NavPress, 2020).
3. Matthew 13:24-30.

NOTES

THE TWENTY-FIRST LETTER
1. Jeff Berryman, *Leaving Ruin: A Novel* (Orange, CA: New Leaf, 2002).

THE TWENTY-SECOND LETTER
1. Ultimately published as *The Jesus Way*.
2. *S. K.*: Søren Kierkegaard.

THE TWENTY-THIRD LETTER
1. Martin Buber, *Israel and the World: Essays in a Time of Crisis* (Syracuse, NY: Syracuse University Press, 1997).
2. Annie Proulx, *The Shipping News: A Novel* (New York: Scribner, 1993).
3. It won both: the National Book Award in 1993, and the Pulitzer Prize in 1994.
4. Marilynne Robinson, *Gilead* (New York: Picador, 2004).
5. Leif Peterson, *Catherine Wheels* (Colorado Springs, CO: WaterBrook, 2005).
6. Eugene is alluding to 1 Kings 19:18 and Romans 11:4.

THE TWENTY-FOURTH LETTER
1. This phrase is found in Psalm 91:6.
2. Ultimately published as *The Jesus Way*.
3. Wallace Stegner, *The Big Rock Candy Mountain* (New York: Penguin Classics, 2010).

THE TWENTY-FIFTH LETTER
1. John 14:5; 20:28.
2. Eugene H. Peterson, *Eat This Book: A Conversation in the Art of Spiritual Reading* (Grand Rapids, MI: Eerdmans, 2006).
3. Eugene H. Peterson, *Tell It Slant: A Conversation on the Language of Jesus in His Stories and Prayers* (Grand Rapids, MI: Eerdmans, 2008).

THE TWENTY-SIXTH LETTER
1. Philip Larkin, "Church Going," in *Philip Larkin Poems: Selected by Martin Amis* (London: Faber & Faber, 2011).
2. *In awkward reverence*: from a part of "Church Going" not quoted above.
3. George Eliot, *Adam Bede* (New York: Penguin Classics, 2008).
4. George Herbert, *The Country Parson: His Character and Rule of Holy Life* (Boston: James B. Dow, 1842), 11.
5. H. Stanley Wood, ed., *Extraordinary Leaders in Extraordinary Times,* vol. 1 (Grand Rapids, MI: Eerdmans, 2006).
6. Eugene here is anticipating Eric's forthcoming sabbatical.

THE TWENTY-SEVENTH LETTER

1. Up until this time, I had kept my relationship with Eugene pretty quiet; I found that my relationships with people were complicated if they knew too soon that I was the son of Eugene Peterson. "Coming out of the closet" here is a reference to when I stopped being so careful about it, having become more confidently established in my personal and pastoral identity in distinction from him.
2. Matthew 25:40, 45.

THE TWENTY-NINTH LETTER

1. Eugene here is referencing N. T. Wright's multiple-volume series *Christian Origins and the Question of God* (Minneapolis: Fortress Press, 1992–2013).
2. Richard Lischer, *The End of Words: The Language of Reconciliation in a Culture of Violence* (Grand Rapids, MI: Eerdmans, 2008).

THE THIRTIETH LETTER

1. As quoted in Deal W. Hudson and Matthew J. Mancini, eds., *Understanding Maritain: Philosopher and Friend* (Macon, GA: Mercer University Press, 1987), 117–118.
2. William P. Young, *The Shack: Where Tragedy Confronts Eternity* (Newbury Park, CA: Windblown Media, 2007).

THE THIRTY-FIRST LETTER

1. Eugene seemed to be in a shorthand mood when writing this letter. To address any confusion: RC = Roman Catholic; HS = Holy Spirit; mss = manuscript; TV = television; ok = okay.
2. SanDisk flash drive.

THE THIRTY-SIXTH LETTER

1. Bill Robinson, *Incarnate Leadership: 5 Leadership Lessons from the Life of Jesus* (Grand Rapids, MI: Zondervan, 2009).
2. Karl Barth, *Letters: 1961–1968* (Grand Rapids, MI: Eerdmans, 1981).
3. Exodus 1:8 and Acts 7:18, KJV.
4. Anne Tyler, *Saint Maybe* (New York: Ivy Books, 1992).

THE THIRTY-SEVENTH LETTER

1. Psalm 21:6, NRSV.

You'll Also Enjoy

LETTERS
— to a —
YOUNG
CONGREGATION

*Nurturing the growth
of a faithful church*

ERIC E. PETERSON

Letters to a Young Congregation is a collection of letters from Eric to the local church he pastored as it came to life. You'll find the message to be universally applicable to other churches, and Pastor Eric's voice to be similar to his father Eugene's— warm, winsome, knowing, and understanding.

CP1601

THE NAVIGATORS® STORY

THANK YOU for picking up this NavPress book! I hope it has been a blessing to you.

NavPress is a ministry of The Navigators. The Navigators began in the 1930s, when a young California lumberyard worker named Dawson Trotman was impacted by basic discipleship principles and felt called to teach those principles to others. He saw this mission as an echo of 2 Timothy 2:2: "And the things you have heard me say in the presence of many witnesses entrust to reliable people who will also be qualified to teach others" (NIV).

In 1933, Trotman and his friends began discipling members of the US Navy. By the end of World War II, thousands of men on ships and bases around the world were learning the principles of spiritual multiplication by the intentional, person-to-person teaching of God's Word.

After World War II, The Navigators expanded its relational ministry to include college campuses; local churches; the Glen Eyrie Conference Center and Eagle Lake Camps in Colorado Springs, Colorado; and neighborhood and citywide initiatives across the country and around the world.

Today, with more than 2,600 US staff members—and local ministries in more than 100 countries—The Navigators continues the transformational process of making disciples who make more disciples, advancing the Kingdom of God in a world that desperately needs the hope and salvation of Jesus Christ and the encouragement to grow deeper in relationship with Him.

NAVPRESS was created in 1975 to advance the calling of The Navigators by bringing biblically rooted and culturally relevant products to people who want to know and love Christ more deeply. In January 2014, NavPress entered an alliance with Tyndale House Publishers to strengthen and better position our rich content for the future. Through *THE MESSAGE* Bible and other resources, NavPress seeks to bring positive spiritual movement to people's lives.

If you're interested in learning more or becoming involved with The Navigators, go to www.navigators.org. For more discipleship content from The Navigators and NavPress authors, visit www.thedisciplemaker.org. May God bless you in your walk with Him!

Sincerely,

DON PAPE
VP/PUBLISHER, NAVPRESS

www.navpress.com

CP1308